START AND RUN A PROFITABLE RESTAURANT
A step-by-step business plan

Michael M. Coltman, M.B.A.

Self-Counsel Press
(*a division of*)
International Self-Counsel Press Ltd.
Canada   U.S.A.

Printed in Canada

First edition: October, 1983; Reprinted: August, 1988
Second edition: May, 1991; Reprinted: April, 1992
Third edition: December, 1993; Reprinted: July, 1995

Canadian Cataloguing in Publication Data

Coltman, Michael M. (Michael MacDonald), 1930-
   Start and run a profitable restaurant

(Self-counsel business series)
ISBN 0-88908-787-3

   1. Restaurant management. I. Title. II. Series.
TX911.3.M27C64   1993   647.95'068   C93-091915-7

Cover photo Gary Ritchie Photography, Vancouver, B.C.

Self-Counsel Press
(*a division of*)
International Self-Counsel Press Ltd.
Head and Editorial Office
1481 Charlotte Road
North Vancouver, British Columbia V7J 1H1

U.S. Address
1704 N. State Street
Bellingham, Washington 98225

CONTENTS

vi

LIST OF SAMPLES

LIST OF WORKSHEETS

PREFACE

Since the first edition of this book was published in 1983, some major lifestyle changes have had a direct impact on the restaurant industry. Consider, for example, the following challenges that face today's restaurant operators:

(a) People are generally more health conscious. They are concerned about what is in their food (for example, what is the fat content of a hamburger?) and about what they eat. This is evident in how salads are now viewed. At one time a salad was treated as an appetizer or accompaniment to an entrée. Today, people enjoy salads as a main course and fast food chains that built their reputations on hamburgers and similar items have added salad bars or packaged take-out salads to their menus.

(b) People are also much more concerned about how their food is prepared. For example, one private group recently placed large advertisements in major newspapers to alert people to the fact that a particular international restaurant chain was cooking its french fried potatoes in beef tallow, a product that is very high in cholesterol.

(c) Tastes are also changing. For example, today's restaurant customers no longer assume "pasta" means spaghetti in a sauce. They expect pasta to be offered in many different forms — and even different colors! Pasta can still be served as a main course, but can also be offered as a side dish or even as part of a salad. Per capita pasta consumption has increased nearly 50% in the last decade.

(d) Concerns about the environment have also had an impact on restaurants. Consumers are requiring restaurants that serve food and beverages in disposable containers to use containers that do not produce chemical by-products during their manufacture and that are also recyclable or biode-gradable. In many jurisdictions there are now legal requirements for the disposal of empty glass and plastic containers.

(e) Changing technology is also affecting restaurants. Electronic sales registers today are far more sophisticated and can provide a great deal more information about product sales and inventory usage than their mechanical predecessors. Another example is customers' use of bank debit cards (rather than credit cards) to pay their restaurant bills. A restaurant can use a device connected to a bank's automated teller machine (ATM) so that a customer presenting a debit card can have the amount deducted from his or her bank account and transferred immediately to the restaurant's bank account. This opens up a new market for restaurants that can capitalize on catering to customers who do not have credit cards and choose not to pay with cash.

(f) Restaurants today in most jurisdictions are also required to provide specialized facilities for people with disabilities. Customers are also demanding that restaurants provide separate smoking and nonsmoking areas.

(g) Finally, because of changing demographics, restaurant operators are facing a shrinking labor pool of younger people and so are turning instead to employing people who have disabilities or who are elderly.

1
INTRODUCTION

Although, in North America, taverns and inns have existed since the earliest times, the first restaurant didn't appear until 1827. In that year, the Swiss-born Delmonico brothers opened a cafe and pastry shop in New York City. The cafe offered pastries, bonbons, fancy ices, and beverages such as coffee, chocolate, wines, and liqueurs.

As their business improved, they opened their first real restaurant in 1832 and introduced the North American public to the idea of dining out. They adapted French cuisine to the abundance of game and crops that North America offered, and the resulting dishes were exquisite. Menus were printed in both French and English, and waiters were also bilingual. Delmonico's restaurants (they soon added others) offered a standard of quality and service at a reasonable price that still stands today. Even though the last Delmonico's restaurant closed in the 1920s, the name is still with us today in the Delmonico steak.

Despite Delmonico's success, and the success of many other restaurants since that time, you may find this introductory chapter a bit discouraging. This is done deliberately since too many novices go into the restaurant business oblivious to the pitfalls. If this chapter does nothing more than make you more wary, then it has achieved its objective.

a. REASONS FOR GOING INTO THE RESTAURANT BUSINESS

Please tick off whichever of the following are the reasons you know you'll be successful in the restaurant business:

(a) I like food.

(b) I often eat in restaurants and know good food.

(c) I make a great carrot cake.

(d) My parents always wanted me to be a great chef.

(e) I worked as a busperson in a restaurant while going to high school.

(f) My spouse is a great cook and will be the chef.

(g) I know someone named Delmonico who will be my chef.

(h) I have this secret recipe I got from a restaurant in Europe.

(i) I know why other restaurants didn't make it.

(j) There's this restaurant down the street that went broke and the rent is only . . . .

(k) Most restaurants don't open for breakfast.

(l) I'll specialize in . . . (fill in the empty space).

(m) Everybody likes Greek (or insert your own ethnic choice) food.

(n) I'll beat the competition with lower prices.

(o) Running a restaurant is no different from any other business.

(p) I grow special herbs in my garden.

(q) I won't allow tipping.

(r) I was successful in a hardware store.

(s) I love barbecuing.

(t) I took a Cordon Bleu course by correspondence.

If even a single one of the above reasons is your prime motivation for going into the restaurant business, you may be in trouble from the start.

In a free enterprise society, it is anyone's right to go into business just as it is often their privilege to close up shop — sometimes in bankruptcy. One business where going broke is easier than any other is the restaurant business. Walk down any block in any reasonably large town where restaurants are likely to be and you will probably see one or more buildings with signs in the window proclaiming "Opening soon under new management" or "Closed for renovations." The chances are that, before those signs appeared, a restaurant operated unsuccessfully, and another one is going to open there soon.

The restaurant business in most cities is spread so thinly that for any new restaurant to open, another one must have gone broke. However, there always seems to be another entrepreneur to take over and risk life savings in the restaurant business.

1. Investment cost

To put up a restaurant building on owned land can cost anywhere from $500,000 to $1,000,000. You don't finance a million-dollar restaurant with its high risks by only having savings of $10,000 or $20,000. For that reason the main emphasis in this book will be on renting space for your restaurant. If you do plan to build, chapter 7 examines some of the major concerns.

Even taking over leased premises, purchasing necessary restaurant equipment and furniture, and making leasehold improvements can require as much as $350,000. If you have to finance 70% to 75% of that, the debt service charges (interest and repayment of principal) may put you in the poorhouse before you can start making a reasonable return on your own investment.

2. Return on investment

Successful restaurants, very successful ones, might make as much as 20 cents profit on each sales dollar. A reasonably successful one might make 10 cents. The average restaurant that manages to survive might make 3 to 5 cents; but when that 3 to 5 cents is related to the amount of money the owner invested, it might end up being less than the amount that could have been earned in interest by leaving the money in the bank. And money in the bank requires no hard work, long hours, or high risk.

3. High risk

The risk in the restaurant business is high. In North America, about one-third of all restaurants in business today will turn over within a year. Within three years, 50% of them will be out of business. Only 20% will survive to their fifth anniversary.

The independent restaurant operator has even more of a struggle than the operator who is part of a chain or franchise. Also, if you have a dream of owning your own restaurant and letting someone else run it for you, beware! More than one absentee owner has gone broke because he or she has allowed the manager to lose money.

Other absentee owners think that you make money out of liquor so the food operation doesn't matter. A liquor license is not a right to print money. For example, "salting the bar" is a classic rip-off by bartenders who bring in their own bottles of liquor, sell the contents, make no record of the sales, and pocket the cash. You'll never know the difference if you're not around to see what's happening.

b. TYPICAL PROBLEMS

Despite all this, the restaurant business might still be for you if you can handle the following:

(a) Suppliers who cannot deliver the quality of goods you want (and in some cases are paying for) but continue to expect you to do business with them

(b) Suppliers who change their prices drastically without notice and can't understand why you can't change your menu prices just as quickly

(c) Suppliers who deliver aged sheep despite the fact your menu advertises "spring lamb"

(d) Customers who blame you because they forgot to ask you to validate their parking tickets and only remembered after they got to the parking lot after dinner

(e) Customers who make reservations but don't show up (meanwhile you've turned away a party of eight and have lost $200 in sales)

(f) Customers who show up half an hour late for a reservation and wonder why you don't now have a table available

(g) Customers who ask you to improve the quality of your decor and/or menu and/or service but don't want to pay for it in higher prices

(h) Customers who never ask for particular items on your menu, but complain bitterly when you no longer list them

(i) Customers who would just shrug their shoulders if the stove repairman couldn't show up until three days hence to fix their home appliance, but who insist that, despite all your problems, you never fail to be ready for lunch and dinner (and even breakfast) promptly at your advertised time

(j) Customers who complain if you use convenience foods such as frozen strawberries in mid-winter at your restaurant in Alaska

(k) Health inspectors who ignore the fact that you meticulously follow all proper sanitary procedures in food storage, preparation, and service and criticize you because there's a single cracked tile on the kitchen floor

(l) Cooks who believe they are part of a sacred sect and insist that cooking is an art but haven't got a clue about organizing their own kitchens to create a harmonious, productive working environment

(m) Cooks who don't feel it's their responsibility (even though they insist you let them run the kitchen) to reduce opportunities for loss, theft, and inefficiency

(n) Bartenders and waiters/waitresses who, because they face the public, can do more to sink your business than anyone but feel they have no need to be polite, attentive, and neat and tidy

(o) Governments who treat you like second-class citizens

(p) Governments who require you to keep a larger inventory of paper records than food and beverage supplies

(q) Restaurant reviewers who use pressure tactics on behalf of their publication's advertising departments

All of the above problems are part of the main course. If you want to be in the restaurant business, you have to learn to live and cope with them.

Also, from the public's point of view, the problems are not all as one-sided as they seem. There are restaurant operators without taste, talent, or honesty. Some of them are unreasonably successful, probably because too many restaurant patrons know nothing different.

c. CHARACTERISTICS FOR SURVIVAL

Suppose you read the following in the help wanted section of your local newspaper:

Worker wanted for new business. Must like hard work and interaction with public. No previous experience necessary. Responsible for business 24 hours a day, 7 days a week. Duties, in addition to overall management, include purchasing, receiving, inventory control, bookkeeping, hiring, personnel, payroll, maintenance and janitorial, government relations, advertising and public relations, insurance, menu design, cooking, serving, cashiering, control, food/health/tax regulations, credit, sales, customer complaints. No vacation for first 3 years. Salary will depend on profits. Some risk of losing possessions such as car, furnishings, personal residence, and spouse and family leading to permanent paranoia.

If this ad were run by a large company, you probably wouldn't even bother applying, but the conditions outlined above are typical of the restaurant business.

Numerous studies have been conducted to determine the characteristics of a successful restaurant entrepreneur. However, there is no general consensus about what constitutes the right blend of characteristics. What is important in one individual may be less important in another. In general, though, the following characteristics, to a greater or lesser extent, and in some combination, appear to be important:

(a) Drive or energy and the willingness to take responsibility and risks, make decisions, and accept the consequences

(b) Personal initiative and the ability to not rely on others to get the ball rolling or defer decisions to others or to committees

(c) Personality and human relations ability. This includes emotional stability, sociability, cheerfulness in adversity, cooperation, tact, and consideration for others.

(d) Organizational ability with an eye to detail so that those around you don't have to guess what needs to be done and who has to do it

(e) Communication ability both written and oral. You have to be able to communicate with employees, suppliers, customers, bankers, and all the other people you have to deal with daily.

(f) Administrative ability in planning, setting goals and objectives, deciding how to measure results, controlling the business, interpreting financial statements, and similar matters

(g) Technical knowledge about the restaurant business. This means not only knowing what you do know but also where you may be deficient in certain skills and technical abilities so that you can upgrade yourself or hire employees competent in that area.

(h) Good judgment, patience, and restraint

(i) Leadership

Looking over that list you might think that nobody could ever survive in the restaurant business. However, this is only a list of desirable characteristics that are helpful in most situations, it is not necessarily indicative of failure if you don't possess one or several of them.

1. Willingness to work hard

One characteristic is generally absolutely essential: a willingness to work hard. Without that, you are almost certainly doomed to fail in the restaurant business.

If you do work hard, you should achieve success. That success will be measured not only in having a profitable restaurant, but also in the rewards that are less easy to measure, such as being your own boss, having pride in restaurant ownership, enjoying status in the community, and owning an outlet for creative ideas.

2. Other questions

Now, honestly answer the following questions:

(a) Do I have the mental and physical stamina to run my own restaurant?

(b) Am I prepared to sacrifice my present lifestyle to this new venture?

(c) Are my spouse and family (if any) willing to accept the change and possible upheaval in lifestyle?

(d) How much income do I need to survive during this period of change?

(e) Can I survive if all my income has to come from a new restaurant venture that may or may not be successful?

If the answer to each of these five questions is not a definite yes, it is possible you may be acting on emotion rather than in an objective way. In that case, if you do not succeed, you have only yourself to blame.

d. ADVANTAGES AND DISADVANTAGES OF STARTING A NEW RESTAURANT

The main emphasis in this book will be on starting a new restaurant from scratch. There are both advantages and disadvantages to starting a new restaurant, and you might want to be aware of these in order to consider the alternative of purchasing an already existing restaurant that is for sale.

1. Advantages

Some of the advantages of starting your own restaurant are as follows:

(a) You can select a location that takes advantage of current economic or market conditions.

(b) If your plans include constructing a new building, you can have it designed to your specifications to suit the type of restaurant you plan to have, and the type and size of building can also be designed for conditions as they exist today.

(c) There may be an appeal to potential customers about a new restaurant being opened. Curiosity alone may help you attract a good starting clientele.

(d) You can start a restaurant suited to current trends in dining out, using suitable decor, menu, and service.

2. Disadvantages

Some of the disadvantages of starting your own business are as follows:

(a) If land and building are involved, the time required to put together a financing arrangement to buy the necessary land and put together a building package can be long and the financing itself fairly complex.

(b) A clientele will have to be built up. This takes time — anywhere from a few months in some restaurants to two to three years in others. Starting a new restaurant does not, by itself, create an immediate new clientele or market.

(c) Building up a clientele also delays a return on your own investment, and during this time interest will have to be paid on borrowed money. In addition, it may require you to keep advancing the company new cash to keep it in operation.

(d) Any new restaurant suffers an additional risk since it will probably have to compete with already existing competitive restaurants whose sites and/or locations are more favorable and whose business is already successfully established.

If you feel that the above disadvantages outweigh the advantages, you should then seriously consider the alternative of purchasing an already successful restaurant business. If that is the case, you might wish to combine the information in this book with the information in *Buying and Selling a Small Business*, another title in the Self- Counsel Series. Another alternative might be to try to reduce the risk by starting your restaurant on a franchised basis. Franchising is discussed in chapter 14.

2
WHAT KIND OF RESTAURANT IS FOR YOU?

One of the earliest decisions you are going to have to make is the type of restaurant you wish to operate.

a. RESTAURANT TYPES

Restaurants can be difficult to classify, but the following broad, general classifications might help you narrow your decision.

1. Family or commercial

Family restaurants generally offer a wide menu selection of the "meat and potatoes" type with a medium price range. If licensed, the license is usually restricted to beer and wine. Decor is bright, and a combination of counters, tables, and booths is common.

Parking is a necessity since customers (the family unit) generally arrive by car. Price range of the menu items has to appeal to the average family income. Location is important as is proximity to a residential area with good highway access. High traffic volume may be critical.

Operating hours are generally from early morning to midnight. Chain and franchise restaurants, where reputation attracts repeat business, are often successful operations. Staff are generally friendly and efficient, but not necessarily highly trained. Investment is medium to high.

2. Coffee shop

The coffee shop is characterized by fast food service and high seat turnover. Seating is often limited to counter service. Decor is minimal, and prices are relatively low.

Prime locations are office buildings or shopping malls with high pedestrian traffic volume. As a result, rent may also be high. Staff are often minimally trained.

Peak periods are lunch and coffee breaks, with some breakfast business possible. Hours may run from early morning to early evening, and sometimes to midnight. Take-out business may be offered.

3. Cafeteria

Cafeterias require large traffic volumes. Location can be critical to encourage this volume. Shopping centers and office buildings are good locations. Self-service is typical in cafeterias with menus somewhat limited but covering soups, entrées, desserts, and beverages.

Cafeterias often require large preparation areas. Staff are minimally trained. Beer and wine may be offered. Speed of service is essential to handle the traffic volume. Hours will depend on the location (for example, school, industrial plant, office building).

4. Gourmet

Gourmet restaurants generally require a higher investment than the others discussed so far. They require an ambience and decor that costs money. This type of restaurant caters to those who require a higher standard and are willing to pay for it. Success depends on establishing a reputation that will attract repeat business.

Prices are higher because of the investment required and because of the reduced seat turnover. Food and beverage offerings must be carefully selected because of the clientele. A good variety of wines is essential. Staff must be highly trained.

Even though the lunch trade is important to such restaurants, the evening period is often where the emphasis is placed, with leisurely dining an advertising feature.

5. Ethnic

Ethnic restaurants feature the foods of a specific region or country. Ethnic restaurants can run the gamut from family (e.g., Chinese) to gourmet (e.g., classical French) cuisine. Decor fitting the ethnic motif is important, as is menu design, staff uniforms, and training.

To be successful, ethnic restaurants must serve authentic food, which means food preparation staff must be well trained and knowledgeable. Price range can be from budget to elevated. Beer, wine, and liquor may or may not be served. Investment may be high because of decor and staff training.

Location can be variable, and the emphasis is on evening meals, although luncheon business with lower prices is not precluded.

6. Fast food

Fast food restaurants have mushroomed in the past 20 years as people have become more mobile. Franchising is prevalent in this type of restaurant. These restaurants can be eat-in or take-out, or a combination of both.

The menu is limited, and prices are relatively low. You can choose one particular kind of food to feature. For example, ethnic food of one type or another can be sold in a fast food format. Because of low prices, a high traffic volume (pedestrian and/or automobile) is critical.

A fast food restaurant has to stay open long hours, and generally seven days a week. Alcoholic beverages are not usually offered. Staff training may not be highly critical unless it is a franchise operation where the franchisor generally sets standards of service and food quality that must be maintained at all times.

7. Delicatessen

Delicatessen food service, marrying traditional delicatessen cold meats and cheeses with take-out sandwiches, salads, and similar items are now quite popular. Some delis may also have limited seating.

Delis are generally located in traditional "shopping" areas or office buildings and therefore are usually open from 9 a.m. to 5 p.m. or 9 a.m. to 9 p.m. Take-out items are limited, and capital investment is relatively low. This type of restaurant is low in labor cost since only one or two owners/employees may be involved.

8. Buffet

A buffet restaurant is usually established as a completely self-serve operation. However, if liquor, beer, and wine are offered, table service for these beverages is necessary.

The food buffet is usually an "all you can eat" hot and cold food one-price operation. Food preparation and service staff can be kept to a minimum. This type of restaurant caters primarily to the family trade, so prices must be reasonable. Although lunch may be offered, prime business is from 5 p.m. to 11 p.m.

Location is important since plenty of nearby parking must be available. Banquet and catering facilities may also be part of the restaurant operation.

9. Institution

Institutional restaurants are most common in office buildings. They are usually cafeteria style. Operating hours are often established by the company or building owners.

Equipment may be owned by the company or building owner, who may also pay expenses such as utilities and maintenance. However, the cost of these may be built into the rent you pay.

Prices must be kept low, and may even be subsidized (as an employee benefit) in a company restaurant. Operators of institutional restaurants often have a built-in or even captive market; but they are required to adhere to levels of quality and other conditions imposed by the landlord.

It may be difficult for the novice restaurateur to pick up an institutional contract since such contracts are normally offered to operators with a proven track record.

However, consider this type of operation for the future since profits can be relatively high and stable.

10. Coffee bar

One of the most recent and fast-growing segments of the restaurant business is the coffee bar. These establishments specialize in high-quality coffee as well as specialty coffees (such as espresso, cappuccino, and latté) for on-site or take-out consumption. Some food items might also be offered such as muffins and donuts.

To supplement revenue, coffee bars also sell high-grade coffee beans, items such as coffee-making equipment, and mugs. Space requirements and capital investment for a coffee bar are minimal because only a coffee production and serving counter is needed. Some seating may be offerred both inside and outside. Limited staff training is required. Coffee bars often operate with extended hours (e.g., 6 a.m. to midnight).

Coffee bars are generally located in busy retail shopping areas where there is a high pedestrian level.

11. Landlord's decision

Note also that the type of restaurant is often dependent on the landlord. Most landlords (particularly those in shopping malls) who have a good location for a restaurant seek out highly qualified and financially secure tenants who will operate a certain type of restaurant. This is generally why chain and/or franchise restaurants often operate in these prime locations.

b. THE NEXT STEP

Once you are fairly sure of the type of restaurant you wish to operate, you can take the next step — that is, to seek out restaurants of the type you are considering and begin assessing them. This simply means visiting them as a regular customer and viewing them from the customer's point of view.

This point of view needs to be objective. Ask yourself these questions: What hours are they open? What is the traffic volume? Are there peaks and valleys of demand? What is the price range? What are the menu offerings? What type of customers are served? Do they seem generally satisfied? How many seats are there? Is that too many or too few based on customer counts?

1. A feel for the business

The answers to these questions will give you a better feel for the nature of the business you are going into. You can also confirm in your own mind the type of restaurant you would like to have.

Sometimes, it may be a good idea to talk to the restaurant's employees and/or owners. Make sure you do this at a slow business time. However, if you do talk to restaurateurs, you'll find that none of them has any problems. The one with the problems is the operator down the street. The only trouble is, when you talk to the one down the street, he or she will tell you the restaurateur with the problems is the one you just talked to. Restaurateurs tend to exaggerate, particularly if they think you are a potential purchaser of their business.

2. Talk to failures

Talk to restaurateurs who have failed, since a lot of survivors survive by accident rather than by knowing their product and their market and using a businesslike approach to success.

You can obtain names of failures from suppliers to the restaurant industry, such as food wholesalers (for example, meat packers). Real estate companies, banks, and liquor and health inspectors may also provide you with names of failures.

Learn from their reasons for failure. Often, the reason will be that the owner knew too little about the business. Many ex-restaurateurs are bartenders who knew how to mix the best martini in the world, or chefs who had a recipe from the Ritz, or fast food restaurant managers whose success was handed to them in a franchised formula restaurant.

All these people may have succeeded in their specific area of the business, but they didn't understand all the varied aspects of the business well enough to succeed as the owner of their own operation.

A successful restaurant operator does not know just the bar business, or the kitchen, or fast food operations, but understands that there are many complex aspects of the business that must be handled well to make a restaurant successful. If you lack skill in any one of them, you either have to learn that aspect in a hurry or hire someone who understands and can implement it.

3. Ease of entry

The restaurant business is too easy to get into. If you want to become a used car dealer, or run a retail store, you'll have great difficulty since the people who lend you money generally insist that you have some experience in the business before they will become your creditor. But for some reason no restaurant authority or association insists that you put up a certain amount of money yourself, or that you understand what working capital is, or that you write an exam to prove competence. It's a business that almost anyone can get into with the greatest of ease, and for the same reason it is a business that anyone can fail at — also with the greatest of ease.

For that reason, the more you can find out about what makes for success in the restaurant business the more likely you are to succeed. This discovery process might even include, if you haven't already done so, working in a restaurant to view things from inside.

c. WHERE TO FIND RESTAURANTS FOR SALE

If, after all this, you are satisfied you are making the right move, you can begin to become more specific by talking to restaurant owners whose business is for sale. You should do this even if you plan to start your own restaurant rather than buying an existing one.

The easiest way to find out what is for sale is to scan the classified ads in your local newspaper under the Business Opportunities section. If your community is typical of most, you will probably find that 50% of these advertisements are related to restaurants.

Another way to find out if restaurants are for sale is to simply walk or drive around the area where you might like to locate. Even if you do not see any "for sale" signs, there is no harm in approaching restaurant operators located there anyway. You might at least prompt them to think about selling.

You can visit the restaurants that appeal to you and talk to the owners. Find out exactly what is offered for the price. Is it land, building, furniture, and equipment? Or only building, furniture, and equipment? More than likely it will only be furniture and equipment or even, in some cases, merely the "goodwill" for the remaining life of the restaurant's lease, since the landlord also owns the furniture and equipment.

What is the owner's price for what is being sold? How many square feet or seats are involved? Convert the asking price to a cost per square foot or cost per seat to get a more concrete idea of what it is going to cost you to start your own restaurant. You will also get a firm idea of current prices if you do decide to buy an existing restaurant.

1. Real estate companies

Some real estate sales companies specialize in, or have employees who specialize in, restaurants and other commercial properties. Note that the sales agent in this case is primarily concerned with obtaining the best deal for the seller and that his or her income depends on making a sale. Sales agents' advice must therefore be considered with this in mind. Try to determine if the agent's statement about why the business is for sale matches what you can find out from other sources (such as the res-taurant's employees or its sup-

pliers). The sale price of a business sold via an agent may also be higher because the vendor is likely to include the agent's commission in the selling price.

Finally, note that if an existing restaurant owner seems too eager to sell, or if what seems like an excellent location is available on which to build a new restaurant, you might question why a franchise or chain operation has bypassed that opportunity. Leasing agents and site developers traditionally offer opportunities to franchisors and/or chain operations before considering independent entrepreneurs. If a sales agent is involved, how forceful the agent is can also be an indication of how viable that location may be for a restaurant.

3
YOUR MENU

You may wonder why a chapter about your menu appears so early in this book. Many new restaurateurs assume the menu can be prepared after everything else has been arranged. Surprisingly, that is not true. In fact, your menu is the foundation of your restaurant; many other factors depend on it.

a. TYPE OF RESTAURANT AND THE MENU

The type of restaurant you plan to operate can dictate in part the type of menu you must have. This is particularly true of ethnic restaurants where the people you serve expect to see certain items they are familiar with on the menu.

Commercial and family restaurants also tend to offer common items that customers expect. However, even in cases where your restaurant type dictates certain menu items, you still have flexibility in other menu items. For example, even a seafood restaurant has to offer alternatives such as chicken for those who are not seafood eaters.

1. General menu requirements

In general terms, your menu needs to be balanced, nutritious, and varied. This balance must also consider what your customers are likely to want, and not just what you think they should have.

Important aspects of menu composition are the texture, flavor, and color of food, complementary food items (potato, vegetable, salad), garnishes, and aroma, taste, and appearance. The way you put together all these tangible and intangible ingredients is going to decide in large part whether or not you will have customers.

2. Menu presentation

Your written or printed menu creates the first impression about what you offer, your range of offerings, and your selling prices. This may well attract customers into your restaurant; but it is the sense of satisfaction, of having received value for money from your food offerings, as well as the service received, that is going to bring customers back.

Keep this in mind when you choose your menu design, printing type, size, and colors. You want a menu that reflects the style and theme of your restaurant. For example, some smaller restaurants with menu items limited by season, availability, etc., find it easier to write the daily menu on a blackboard. This way, customers aren't irritated by being told that an item they want isn't available that day.

One concern about a printed menu is the cost. With food costs always rising, you need to adjust your menu prices from time to time. Don't spend so much money on a fancy menu that it will have to be re-done before it has paid for itself.

The size of the menu can also be important. For example, a larger sized menu allows you to display more prominently menu items that you wish to feature because they are more profitable to sell. On the other hand, the larger the menu size, the higher its production and printing costs.

Menu descriptions are generally best if they are short and descriptive. Menus with pages and pages about each item can intimidate customers. Also, don't get carried away with your descriptions. If you advertise fresh vegetables, or fresh fruit, make sure they *are* fresh.

3. Other menu considerations

Other considerations when you are deciding what to feature on your menu are product availability and seasonality in your area. You must also weigh industry trends and decide whether they are dictated by short-term customer fads or more permanent long-term trends.

Another factor is the need to adhere to government regulations in your jurisdiction. These regulations may require you to state on your menu whether sales tax is included in the selling price of menu items or is added to the items' prices. Regulations may also require you to adhere to truth in advertising laws. For example, these laws do not allow you to list one thing on your menu but actually substitute something else — such as stating that you deep fry shrimp in peanut oil when in fact you are using beef fat to save money. This is not only illegal, but may also lead to a lawsuit if a customer is allergic to beef fat and becomes ill.

b. EFFECT OF MENU ON PRE-OPENING DECISIONS

Your menu will affect a number of your major pre-opening decisions. Some of the more important ones are listed here.

1. Location

Your menu can dictate your location, and vice versa. For example, if you are going to open a Greek restaurant, it might not work too well on a busy highway. There just may not be enough people passing by who want Greek food. You might be wiser to consider locating in an area where there is a large ethnic Greek population to draw on.

On the other hand, if you decide on a location in a Greek community with a lower than average income level, then a Greek "gourmet" restaurant featuring "escargots a la grecque" would be inappropriate.

2. Building

Your menu can affect the size of building you require. A short-order take-out restaurant will require considerably less space than a sit-down restaurant. But even sit-down restaurants require different amounts of space.

A cafeteria that has a limited menu may require less food preparation area than a gourmet restaurant with an extensive menu. This, in turn, affects seating area. A cafeteria may only require 10 to 12 square feet of seating area per customer, whereas a fancy dining room may require 15 to 20 square feet.

3. Equipment

Your menu directly affects your equipment needs and thus the investment required. Generally, the more extensive the menu, the more varied your equipment will need to be. If all you are selling is hamburgers, hot dogs, fries, and soft drinks, your equipment requirements are minimal compared to a restaurant with 20 or 30 menu items requiring a variety of different cooking methods and possibly even some specialized equipment.

If your investment budget is limited, you will probably have to simplify your menu to fit what you can afford to invest in equipment, furnishings, decor, and table settings.

4. Service

Your menu, combined with the type of restaurant you plan to run, usually dictates the level of service you will offer. In a cafeteria, or fast food take-out restaurant, the customers expect to provide their own pick-up service.

However, in a family, commercial, or gourmet restaurant, customers expect to be served at their tables. The more items you have on your menu, the more complex this service can be. A group of four seated at a table, each ordering a different appetizer, entrée, and dessert, requires 12 different items to be ordered, prepared, served, and charged for. In other words, your menu can determine the number of staff required and the cost of staff training for food preparation and service.

Thus, your menu has a direct impact on your labor cost. For example, fast food restaurants have menus that allow them to employ lower-skilled employees who are often hired at minimum wage, whereas a gourmet restaurant's menu will require employees who have more experience, knowledge, and skills in food preparation and table service and who expect to be compensated with higher pay.

The cost of uniforms is also determined by your menu. A standard, general menu served in a commercial or family dining room does not call for service employees to be dressed in anything other than neat, clean, relatively low-cost uniforms. However, in a fancy gourmet restaurant, with expensive decor and menu prices to match, you must provide uniforms that conform to that ambience. This can be expensive.

5. Purchasing methods

Your menu has a direct impact on your purchasing requirements and practices. For example, if you plan to serve steak, you must consider how each type of steak is to be ordered. In other words what grade, size, and specific cut is needed? How will steaks be purchased (fresh or frozen), and how will they be stored before using?

What accompanying items (potato, vegetable, salad, garnish) will there be? Is there a ready year-round source for all these items? If your potato is to be served baked, will you serve sour cream, chopped chives, bacon bits, etc. with it? Will bread be served? If so, what type, how will it be served (hot, cold, presliced)? If small

loaves are served, what quality of serving board and cutting knife will you need?

Will your menu require you to purchase more or less convenience food? (Convenience foods are those partly or wholly prepared by the supplier.) For example, if you are going to specialize in soups, will you purchase convenience food soup bases or prepare all your soups on the premises from fresh ingredients?

Your menu, and its purchasing requirements, also affect your storage requirements. Storage can be dry (packaged and canned goods), refrigerated (dairy, vegetable products), and freezer.

If you plan to use a great deal of precooked and packaged frozen items, your storage requirements may tip in favor of more freezer space and less dry and refrigerated space. You will also need less total food preparation area for meat cutting and menu item preparation. The reduced requirement for square footage translates into less investment required.

6. Food cost

The largest single cost for a restaurant is the food. Your menu reflects directly on this cost. Food cost is the price *you* pay for food in relation to the price you sell it for. The ratio of food cost to retail sales is expressed as a percentage.

The more you pay for menu items, the higher your selling prices will have to be. If the market you plan to serve is not willing to pay those high prices, any reductions in selling prices will reduce your potential profits. The alternative is to buy lower quality products of the same item (if they are available) or reduce the size of the portions you plan to serve to compensate for a reduced selling price. Will your customers accept this lower quality and/or portion size?

One important point to remember when calculating your food cost: no matter how accurate you are, it won't help if you have a competitor down the street who is offering the same item for a greatly reduced price. You can never ignore what the competition is doing, no matter how good you believe your product to be. Chapter 16 explains how to calculate your food cost and maintain controls over your system.

7. Alcoholic beverages

Finally, depending on the laws in your area and for your type of restaurant, your menu is going to dictate the kind of alcoholic beverages you serve. For some restaurants, this is not a problem. People do not generally expect to buy alcoholic beverages in a fast food, or deli, limited menu restaurant.

They might expect to find beer and wine, and possibly even liquor, in a commercial or family cafeteria, coffee shop, or dining room.

Certain ethnic restaurants may require some kinds of alcoholic beverage to be available for reasons of tradition if for no other. However, in most sit-down and gourmet restaurants, alcoholic beverages of all kinds are a requirement. Indeed, for gourmet restaurants, you will need to offer a good, and possibly wide ranging, selection of wines.

The extent of your alcoholic beverage service will require space allocations for storage, preparation (if cocktails are offered), and service. In fact, in some situations where you have a liquor area separate from the dining area, a fully-equipped cocktail bar will be required.

All of this is going to affect your investment, not only in space and equipment, but also in inventory. An extensive wine list means that you must have those wines available, and this can run into thousands, or even tens of thousands, of dollars. (See chapter 16 for more on liquor control.)

8. In summary

This discussion of your menu and its impact on your restaurant is introduced at this point to alert you to the many factors that you must keep in mind as you progress through the following chapters.

It's far too early for you to rush out and buy a blackboard and chalk to write out your menu for your Bohemian bistro or start planning details of your 15-page menu and wine list with your printer. However, keep your menu in mind and begin planning and adjusting for it so that you don't end up, for example, with a bank of six deep fat fryers in your kitchens and not a single item on your menu requiring frying.

If you want to do some research and study in menu composition, some excellent books have been written on the subject. Check to see what is available at your local library. If you are near a school that teaches culinary arts or has a program in hotel/food service management, try the school's library or bookstore.

The following are some books written specifically about restaurant menus:

(a) *Menus: Analysis and Planning* by Lothar A. Kreck. (New York: Van Nostrand Reinhold, 1984).

(b) *Menu Pricing and Strategy* by Jack E. Miller. (New York: Van Nostrand Reinhold, 1987).

(c) *Menu Design, Merchandising and Marketing* by Albin G. Seaberg. (New York: Van Nostrand Reinhold, 1983).

4
CHOOSING YOUR BUSINESS ORGANIZATION AND GETTING THE HELP YOU NEED

Once you have decided to open a particular type of restaurant, one of the earliest decisions that you have to make is the legal organizational form your restaurant will have. After that, you will want the help of various professionals to get you started. The three common types of organization are the proprietorship, the partnership, and the limited company.

a. PROPRIETORSHIP

The easiest way for you to establish an organization with little or no cost or legal work is to operate as a proprietorship. Many restaurants are operated this way, with the owner responsible for the actions and liabilities of the restaurant, even if the day-to-day running of it is delegated to others.

As a proprietorship, you would be financed primarily from your personal savings and possibly from bank loans and, if the restaurant is successful, from the profits of the restaurant reinvested in it. The profit of the proprietorship is the personal income of you the owner and is taxed, with any salary paid to you by the restaurant, at personal tax rates. Any loans from creditors or investors are made to you as owner and not to the company.

Businesses established as proprietorships must conform to local regulations in order to, for example, obtain a license to legally operate as a restaurant.

The main advantage of a proprietorship is that, as owner, you have total control of the restaurant and will reap the full financial rewards. There are also minimal legal restrictions on a proprietorship, and it can be easily discontinued if and when you want to get out of the restaurant business.

There are a few disadvantages to the proprietorship. Theoretically, the organization ceases to exist when the owner dies, and the assets of the company become part of the owner's estate and are subject to estate and inheritance taxes. Thus, it may be difficult for relatives to continue the restaurant.

A proprietorship may also find it difficult to expand since it does not have the same opportunities to raise capital as do other types of restaurant organizations that have a broader base of financial resources. Also, generally speaking, in a bankruptcy or serious lawsuit, your personal assets (such as your house, car, and personal savings) as well as the restaurant's assets may be seized to satisfy the liabilities of the organization. In other words, the proprietorship's liability is unlimited. This is probably the major disadvantage of a proprietorship.

b. PARTNERSHIP

Unlike the sole proprietorship, the partnership is generally a more formal type of business organization. It is a legal association between two or more individuals or co-owners of a business. Although a partnership does not require a written agreement, all partners probably should agree to a negotiated contract, or articles of partnership.

In a partnership, each partner may represent the restaurant and enter into contracts on its behalf. Each partner is also personally liable for the debts of the restaurant incurred by other partners. This personal liability (as with the proprietorship) is unlimited.

In a partnership the restaurant's net income, or loss, is shared according to the terms of the partnership contract, and each partner includes that share, plus any salary received from the company, on his or her personal tax return.

Partnerships, like proprietorships, do not issue shares of any kind, and must conform to regulatory authorities.

1. Advantages and disadvantages

Partnerships are relatively easy to organize. Financing is sometimes easier to obtain, and the total partnership investment can usually be much greater than in a proprietorship. A partnership may also have a greater depth of combined judgment and managerial skills. However, except in the case of limited partnerships (discussed later), upon one partner's death or withdrawal from the restaurant, the partnership may have to be dissolved and reorganized. This can make it difficult to continue the restaurant's operations.

Another disadvantage of the partnership is that since in many cases all partners may need to be consulted, quick decisions about the restaurant's operations may be difficult to make and serious disagreements can occur. Also, partners are not only responsible for the debts and obligations they have contracted for, but they are also responsible for those contracted by all other partners.

Finally, it may be difficult to remove an incompetent partner or one you don't get along with. Difficulties often arise with partners concerning the direction the restaurant should go and how it should be run. Sometimes considerable interpersonal skills are necessary to overcome these difficulties. Your partnership contract should spell out details of management and policy-making.

2. Limited partnership

A limited partnership has both general partners with unlimited personal liability and limited partners with limited personal liability. The partnership contract should spell out this limited personal liability. It should also indicate the amount that the limited partners have invested.

A limited partnership arrangement is made when limited, or silent, partners wish to invest in a company and obtain a return on their investment without being personally involved in the day-to-day decision-making and operation of the restaurant.

c. LIMITED COMPANY

Many restaurants are organized as limited companies. The limited company, unlike the proprietorship and partnership or limited partnership, is a separate legal entity, with its own rights and duties, that can continue as a separate organization even after the death of an owner. A limited company can be created for any size of restaurant; it is wrong to consider it appropriate only for larger businesses.

Establishing a limited company is both more complex and more costly (from a legal and accounting point of view) than establishing a proprietorship or a partnership. Despite these problems, it is an effective way of operating a business.

For regulatory purposes, a limited company is like a person. It can sue and be sued, just like an individual, and it must conform to regulatory authorities. It is an ongoing organization with an infinite life of its own even though employees and owners come and go. Many of its assets, such as land and buildings, may indeed have a longer life than the life of the shareholders.

Limited companies may be either public or private. A public company is generally one that has its shares listed on a stock exchange. The legal requirements for operating a public company are much more strict than those for a private company. You will more likely be interested in organizing a private limited company since that type of company is designed for the small business operator.

The major advantage of the limited company form of business is that, generally speaking, since the company is a separate legal entity, the individual owner cannot be held responsible for the company's liabilities. The owner, in other words, has a liability limited to his or her investment in shares in the company.

However, despite this, lending institutions that you approach for financing will generally make you sign a personal note to extend your liability outside the protection offered by the company. This is particularly true for a new restaurant.

Another advantage is that financing may be facilitated by the creation of easily transferable certificates of ownership, known as shares, that may be sold to others, including employees of the company. This broadens the base of financing available to the company. The limited liability of share ownership appeals to some investors since it permits ownership, with a potential return on the investment, without involvement in the restaurant's day-to-day operations.

There may also be some personal tax advantages to forming a limited company that make that form of business appealing. Since each individual situation is different, you should consult your accountant for the tax pros and cons of forming a limited company that suits your particular personal situation.

A limited company is subject to more government regulation and form filing than a proprietorship or a partnership —

although this is a small price to pay considering the advantages that incorporation may offer.

Also, double taxation exists for shareholders of limited companies. The corporation pays taxes on its profit at the corporate tax rate. Any after-tax income may be distributed to the individual shareholders as dividends. The individual is then taxed on these dividends at personal tax rates.

d. SUBCHAPTER "S"

In the U.S., you have a tax option known as subchapter "S." A subchapter "S" corporation is a special form of business organization, permitted for tax reporting purposes only, in which the incorporated company, unlike normal incorporated companies, pays no income tax. Instead, the corporate earnings are taxed in the stockholders' hands as if they were partnership income to those stockholders.

An incorporated company that wishes to qualify under subchapter "S" will have restrictions on it concerning number of stockholders and source of earnings. You should find out what those restrictions are when you are preparing your restaurant plan. Since each individual situation is different, consult your accountant for the tax pros and cons in your particular case.

e. PROFESSIONAL HELP

You are going to need some professional help from people like bankers, accountants, lawyers, and possibly other specialists and consultants, when you start your new restaurant.

In order to select professional advisers, you should shop around. Bankers, accountants, and lawyers, just like any business people, are in competition with each other.

Also, even though these professionals (particularly accountants and lawyers) are members of professional associations and are required to be competent in their field, there are degrees of competence, and also degrees of specialization. Do not choose the first one you visit because of a positive impression, even though that first impression can be important in your final decision.

Let each professional know that you are discussing the situation with two or three others. Then they may not charge you for an initial meeting, if it is short, since this may encourage you to stay with them in the long run.

Check with friends who are in business, or even with people you might meet socially or on other business matters, about professionals they could recommend. However, do not choose a professional adviser solely because you know him or her socially. Try to find a lawyer or accountant who is familiar with the type of restaurant you propose to start.

If you plan to locate in a particular area, select your advisers in that area since they will be familiar with local conditions, and they will be easier to visit when visits are necessary.

You will want to know how much you are going to pay for professional advice. Bankers do not normally charge for their time. Their profit is made from the interest rate they charge you for money that you borrow from them, and for the use they can make of any business funds you have on deposit in accounts with them.

Accountants and lawyers usually charge on an hourly basis, or alternatively charge an annual retainer fee for certain ongoing day-to-day advice, with an extra charge for matters that fall outside what is included in the retainer.

Since accountants and lawyers do have a fairly high hourly fee, you should try to limit the amount of time you use them. As much as possible make decisions for yourself and only call on them when a matter to be resolved is critical and where proper professional help is required.

Also, check at the outset what the procedure is for advice. Generally accountants and lawyers, like most business people, prefer to arrange face-to-face meetings with as much advance notice as possible. Finally, they generally prefer not to give advice over the telephone concerning important matters requiring documentation.

1. Banker

For most small restaurants, a local bank branch is likely to be of more help than a big city bank that handles only large accounts.

You should advise your banker of your intention to start a restaurant and keep him or her informed as you make progress.

You should consider your bank not just as place to store money or borrow money, but also as a provider of services like financial advice, credit references, etc.

Your banker will probably be able to provide you with useful information about the restaurant you plan to start. For example, for a restaurant of a particular type your banker probably handles the accounts of other similar restaurants and can help you evaluate the forecasts in your financial plan (to be discussed in more detail in chapter 10).

Once you are in business, it is important to keep your banker informed of the restaurant's progress. This is particularly true if you have borrowed money from the bank. Your banker is interested in having you succeed since you, as a customer of the bank, are a potential source of profit to the bank.

2. Accountant

If you do not have experience or qualifications in accounting, you will need an accountant if for no other reason than to handle your annual tax return. Tax law and tax accounting for business can be quite complex. Few small restaurant owners have the competence or the time to be knowledgeable about all the intricacies of income tax.

This does not mean that you should not try to familiarize yourself with income tax rules and regulations, since that knowledge can be helpful in the day-to-day operation of any business, but a professional adviser in this area is well worth the cost.

An accountant can also help you set up your initial accounting and control system, including design of forms, and help you select equipment like an office calculator or sales register. As well as preparing your periodic financial statements, an accountant can interpret and analyze them for you and advise on growth possibilities for your restaurant when it is well established.

Once your accountant and banker have been selected, they should meet. There are going to be several situations that arise in areas such as financing and tax planning where the two of them need to consult.

3. Lawyer

You will probably need a lawyer as there will undoubtedly be some legal matters to be taken care of. Your lawyer can help you decide which legal form of organization your restaurant should have.

A lawyer can check items such as licensing requirements and rental contracts, as well as make you aware of any special government requirements that may exist for your type of restaurant.

Use a lawyer who will tell you in advance what the cost of legal services will be — even the cost of an initial meeting.

Once your lawyer and accountant have been selected, it might be a good idea to have them get together also, since some of their areas of concern can overlap and you do not want to pay twice for the same advice or time.

4. Consultants

Specialists can advise you in a variety of areas, such as restaurant layout (for example, in kitchen and dining room areas), inventory control, business organization, advertising campaigns, and many similar areas where you need special help at a particular time. Their fees can run from reasonable to unrealistic.

These specialists, since they are not involved in day-to-day operations, can often view your restaurant in a more objective way and give professional advice to help you improve your profits.

A word of caution about some "consultants." There are many who earn more than their advice is worth. There are no licensing, certification, or competency requirements for them, so anyone (even another restaurateur between restaurants) can become a consultant. In particular, be wary of consultants who offer to find you money for a fee based on the amount of money raised — such as 10% of $200,000 that you need, or $20,000. In fact, a reputable lender would probably not lend money if an intermediary were involved for such an exorbitant percentage fee.

You should hire consultants before getting started because if you bring them in after certain decisions have been made, you may decide after you listen to the consultant's advice that those decisions were the wrong ones. This can be costly, both in terms of reversing the decision and requiring more consulting time. Consultants usually charge by the hour, and the fee can range from $50 to $150 an hour.

5. "Free" services

There are also "consultants" who do not charge for their services. Indeed, they are really sales representatives for the company whose products they are trying to sell you. Their advice may be biased and you must carefully investigate and evaluate any claims that they make. One way to do this is to ask them for the names of restaurants that have purchased their products, then visit those locations to evaluate the products and discuss their quality with the restaurant operators.

Sales agents may also offer you a "free" layout and design service for kitchen and dining areas. However, this free service is probably contingent on your buying their products.

If you use their design service but buy your products from other suppliers, you will likely be invoiced for the design service.

5
FINDING A SITE

Once you have settled on the type of restaurant you wish to have, the organizational form it will have, and the advisers you need, you need to seek out a suitable site. In this chapter, it is assumed that the general location of your restaurant has been selected. In other words, you have made a decision about the community or area in which you wish to do business, and you are now down to the choice of a specific site within that location.

You have two choices. You can find a good existing site and plan your restaurant's decor, menu, and prices to fit that site. The other alternative is to know in advance exactly what type of restaurant you want and find a site that fits.

a. IMPORTANCE OF SITE

Site selection can be critical. The objective in site selection is to find a spot that will bring in the greatest number of customers at the lowest cost to you. Sites are often selected because of their proximity to where the restaurant owner lives or because the premises happen to be vacant or the price attractive. Don't fall into this trap unless you have subjected the site to some suitability tests.

1. General suitability

A practical general rule is to select a site that suits the needs of the customers who are the market for your restaurant. You need to be sure of the specifics of the restaurant you are interested in to understand its particular site and market requirements.

Generally, also, since in the restaurant business the customer has to come to your location, you have to be convenient to those customers. You need good pedestrian access, parking and/or public transportation.

Restaurants have three general markets: local people who live or work near the restaurant, temporary residents such as vacationers, business people, or other visitors, and people in transit who stop for a meal while traveling from point A to point B. A restaurant may cater primarily to any one of those groups or to a combination of them.

If the site you settle on already has a large number of restaurants in the area, that can be an asset. Customers will identify it as a dining area and this helps all restaurants as long as they are not too similar.

2. Site specialists

If you are unfamiliar with the market requirements of your particular restaurant, you may want to use a site specialist. The services of site selection companies include analysis of population density, customer profiles, access and traffic flows, the drawing power of other restaurants in the area, visibility of restaurant and signs, the average sale you should have per square foot or seat, and the effect of any nearby competitors or potential new competitors. Note, though, that assessing a commercial site is both complex and tricky. It is more art than science, and even the specialists can be wrong.

Some real estate companies also have sales agents who deal primarily in leasing space and are expert in finding prospective locations and drafting offers to landlords. Usually you would not have to pay a fee for this service because the sales agent receives a commission from the landlord if an agreement is achieved.

3. Some guidelines

Even though you may rely on a site specialist to help with site selection, there are some obvious things that you should be aware of. For example, you would not want to locate in an area populated or frequented by people of a different socio-economic base than you must sell to. A gourmet restaurant in a working area may have difficulty drawing customers.

Similarly, you would not want to have a particular type of restaurant in a residential area that is populated with people whose ethnic background is not oriented to the type of food you will be selling, or locate a restaurant geared to selling to the younger generation in an area inhabited by older married couples.

For some restaurants, corner sites are often most suitable since there are two streams of pedestrian and vehicular traffic.

b. VISIBILITY, ACCESSIBILITY, AND SUITABILITY

Three extremely important aspects of a good site are visibility, accessibility, and suitability. Each of these will be briefly discussed.

1. Visibility

Visibility of the restaurant may be more important to the customer who arrives at your front door by automobile than it is for the pedestrian, but even for the pedestrian it is important.

Poor visibility of a restaurant outlet can be improved by appropriate outdoor advertising signs that can both attract attention and give directions. This is especially true in a site where the restaurant might be surrounded by larger and taller buildings and where such problems as one-way streets and other complications can confuse the customer traveling by car.

2. Accessibility

A second factor in site location is accessibility, again particularly for those arriving by automobile. An ideal situation is where traffic flow in and around the site reduces the effects of such things as left turn restrictions that prevent the motorist from easily approaching the restaurant.

Equally important is knowledge of future street and/or highway changes that could change a desirable access situation into an undesirable one.

If a routing from the main travel stream is difficult, and sign ordinances prohibit providing the motorist with information such as where to turn to reach the restaurant then a large number of potential customers may be lost.

3. Suitability

Even with good visibility and easy access, the suitability of the site is a critical factor. For many restaurants, the greatest site limitation is space for parking. The space required for parking is usually greater than that required for the building.

A rule-of-thumb with parking is that a restaurant with an automobile clientele requires one parking space for each 2 to 2.5 seats, plus additional parking for employees. For example, a busy 100-seat restaurant would thus need 40 to 50 customer parking spaces and may need as many as 15 to 20 additional spaces for employee parking.

If you are looking for land on which to erect a building, you might need answers to the following questions:

(a) Is the site suitable for building expansion? For example, is it reasonably flat and free of rock outcroppings that might be expensive to remove or build around?

(b) Is road frontage adequate?

(c) Is there sufficient soil depth for the building so that large quantities of fill are not required?

Even if you don't have enough money now to buy more land than immediately needed, it might be a good idea to select a site with adjacent land that could be available for purchase for future building expansion.

c. LOCATION FACTORS

Some further questions that you should have the answers to concerning site specifics are as follows:

(a) Is the site suitable with regard to your competition?

(b) Is it in a high traffic area and are neighboring stores doing a good business?

(c) If the competition is inefficient or unaggressive, what impact would an improvement in that inefficiency or aggressiveness do to this site?

(d) If parking is required, is it adequate and conveniently accessible?

(e) If location on a particular side of the street is important, is it on the best side?

(f) Are there any disadvantages to this site? In other words, is there a more suitable site within this general area? For example, if the site is located between a used car lot and a lumberyard, would it be a good spot for a restaurant?

(g) Is the market a stable or growing one? Consider population trends, payrolls, local attitudes.

(h) Is the site dependent on seasonal business (for example, tourism)?

(i) In rented premises is it a high-rent or low-rent area?

(j) Is the rent competitive?

(k) If it is a low-rent area, and your competition is in a high-rent area because of a more suitable site, how are you going to compensate for the low-rent area to attract business?

(l) Are the surrounding buildings in good repair? If they aren't, they may detract from your restaurant.

(m) Is the area safe from vandals and is there good police and fire protection?

(n) Is there sufficient floor space and room for possible expansion?

(o) Can food purchases be easily delivered?

(p) If you have to rely on public transportation, is it adequate and are there stops nearby?

(q) Have any premises on this site ever previously been a restaurant? If so, what services to the premises (such as electrical, heating, ventilation, and air conditioning) are usable as is?

In the restaurant business, size of population and number of competitors in the local trading area can be key considerations in finding a good site. You should do some research and determine the population base for the particular type of restaurant you are interested in and measure this against the number of your competitors to see if there is enough business for all of you. Check with your local Chamber of Commerce or Board of Trade for information about population ratios.

d. DOWNTOWN AND SHOPPING CENTERS

You might also want to compare the pros and cons of a downtown location or a shopping center or mall.

1. Downtown

In a downtown area there are generally more potential customers than in a suburban area. However, what is critical is whether or not these potential customers can be part of your market. If not, then your market must be from people outside the area, in which case traffic and parking considerations are critical. Also, in a downtown area you can expect higher rent and operating costs.

Downtown locations are often not good for evening and Saturday business since suburban dwellers usually prefer to visit their local shopping malls and restaurants rather than drive downtown.

2. Major shopping centers

Major shopping or community centers are distinguished from local shopping malls. Shopping centers serve communities of 20,000 to 200,000 people, and are generally between a 10- and 40-minute drive from residential areas.

Locating in a major shopping center can create decision problems. Shopping centers usually have high rents, but they do generally attract plenty of traffic and potential customers and have good accessibility, plenty of parking, pooled advertising possibilities, and potential for future restaurant growth.

The lead store in a shopping center is usually a department store or supermarket. In the larger centers, there will be two such department stores or supermarkets, one at either end. Prime locations are adjacent to one of these large stores, or at least between them, to ensure the best traffic flow. Shopping centers also have the advantage of being located in a particular area as a result of extensive research by the center developer. However, you must be sure a shopping center is the right location for your type of restaurant.

Shopping centers generally base part of their rent on your sales volume. For this reason, they seek businesses with a potential for high sales volume and charge a rent that is sometimes only affordable by chain or national companies.

New, untested restaurants without any special features to attract more people in general to the center are often discouraged by shopping center managers because such restaurants will have a low or nonexistent credit rating.

In addition, in shopping centers, you may also have to pay a monthly flat fee, or a percentage of your sales, for general shopping center advertising. In some cases, this fee is based on the square foot area of your restaurant. If so, check to see how much is added to your premises' actual square foot area as your share of "common" areas. You might be unpleasantly surprised. Check also to see if there is a shopping center merchants' association and whether or not all tenants must join. If so, how much is the membership fee going to add to your "rent"?

In most shopping centers your hours of operation and other rules are more or less dictated to you. Find out in advance what they are and decide whether or not you can live with them.

3. Neighborhood shopping mall

Neighborhood shopping malls serve local populations of from 5,000 to 20,000 people and are either within walking distance, or a few minutes' drive, from the majority of the population. Your market is generally limited to those living in the immediate area and because parking is often a problem you may have to rely on the walk-in trade. Not all restaurants are suited to that. On the other hand, rent and other costs may be lower.

4. Other considerations

Finally, note that in downtown and shopping mall locations the landlord may impose exclusive and restrictive menu requirements. In downtown buildings (particularly those that are older) the landlord may also require a demolition lease clause. Note also that competitive factors in a downtown core location can change much more quickly than for suburban locations and/or shopping malls.

e. BYLAWS AND SIMILAR PROBLEMS

Before going too far with your new restaurant location, it is best to make sure that all the local bylaws such as zoning restrictions, building codes, fire regulations, and similar laws allow you to operate your restaurant there. For the same reason, any necessary licensing or certification for your restaurant should be checked out.

1. Zoning

Zoning can regulate such matters as size of structure, the percentage of a lot that may have a building on it, proximity to street, parking requirements, the use to which a building may be put, the size and type of outdoor signs permitted, and even population density in the area that may or may not allow your type of restaurant. If zoning does not allow a larger building on the site, or if there are such problems as height restrictions, can a change in zoning (a variance) be obtained from the local government? If you have any doubts, check first with your local government's planning/zoning department. Your lawyer can be helpful in zoning matters.

Zoning can also regulate any or all of the following: fire, health, safety, environment, parking, occupancy, garbage, sewage, loading, energy, signs, liquor, and access for people with disabilities. Zoning and bylaw regulations have become increasingly strict in recent years. For example, fire regulations may require sprinkler systems or automatic fire extinguishers built into kitchen exhaust hoods. In some jurisdictions, no smoking regulations require restaurateurs to provide smoke-free areas in a restaurant. Environmental regulations may require specific garbage handling procedures. Safety regulations may require special emergency exits and lighting. Handicapped access regulations may require you to provide wide doors and special washroom facilities. Restaurants that were in operation before such regulations were introduced may be allowed to be non-complying, but in a new operation, regulations are generally strictly enforced and must be included in plans before building and construction permits are issued.

Parking can sometimes be a problem. Find out if there is any minimum parking space requirement for your restaurant.

Sign ordinances should also be checked to determine if there are any restrictions on type, placement, number, and size of signs.

As a prospective tenant in leased premises you can ask that the landlord (or real estate agent acting on your or the landlord's behalf) determine what the local zoning and bylaw requirements are for a restaurant in that location. If you are planning to build a new restaurant from scratch, the architect will generally determine what the zoning requirements are for the location that you have selected.

Make sure that the information you obtain concerning bylaws and ordinances is up to date since changes do occur in these regulations from time to time.

2. Utilities

Check the suitability of sewers, water mains, and electrical power supplies with the local engineering or public works department. If these services are not adequate, the cost to upgrade them could be prohibitive. For example, not all buildings are wired for 220 volts, but that amount of power is often necessary for a restaurant.

The proximity of connection points for utility services is also important. If these services are several hundred yards away, the cost for extra hookups could be exorbitant.

3. Highways

Talk to the highways department about their future plans for new highways or bypass routes that could severely affect the visibility and accessibility of your business.

For example, if the site is on a two-lane highway that is slated for widening to four lanes, is a divider planned for separating the two halves of the highway? If this is the case, it may make it difficult, if not impossible, for arriving or departing motorists to drive directly in to or out of the property.

If a purchase of land is involved, check the land deed for easements or other restrictions. Are there any buildings on the land that will first have to be demolished? If so, this cost of demolition must be added to the asking price for the land.

4. Property appraisal

If the site selected entails buying a building, or land and building, you should have an appraisal done before making a final commitment. This appraisal will allow you to compare the site with similar properties in the area. If necessary, obtain a second appraisal for confirmation. The money invested in this will ensure that the restaurant is not located on an overpriced, unsuitable site.

Check every aspect of a potential site: roofs, walls, foundations, structural strength, bearing walls, heating, plumbing, electrical wiring, and air-conditioning. For example, you might find that the building was rewired some years ago, that the wiring was never inspected, and the code has now changed requiring extensive rewiring.

The money you invest to have a competent person inspect your site will be worth it, particularly if it is discovered that the building has 20 years of deferred maintenance! In that case, you might be better off looking at other sites.

f. SUMMARY

In selecting a site observe the situation, talk to other merchants in the area, and check for any increasing trend of bankruptcies in the general area. Find out if there is a local merchants' association. If there is, attend one or two meetings to find out the concerns of local merchants and see who the leaders are so that you can talk to them.

Selecting the right site involves skill, common sense, knowledge, good judgment, and an awareness of the requirements of a successful restaurant such as traffic patterns and circulation, business generators, building planning, real estate, and — probably as important as anything — luck.

6

RENTING PREMISES AND EQUIPMENT

As a restaurateur, chances are you will start your new business in leased or rented premises. The last thing you should consider doing when starting a new restaurant (unless you have a lot of money to invest) is buying land and constructing a building or buying land and/or an existing building. In fact, some money lenders will not lend to new restaurateurs for the purchase of such assets.

Generally, most first-time business owners invest far too much money in bricks and mortar (the building) when they should be leasing that asset, particularly in the early days. To a lesser degree the same is true of equipment and fixtures.

It is in these early years that the risk is often the greatest, and you may not be able to afford the heavy mortgage debt load that owning land and/or a building and expensive equipment obliges. In fact, many leases can be arranged that allow you a later purchase option.

a. LAND AND BUILDING LEASE

A lease is basically a partnership agreement between the landlord (the owner of the land and/or building) and the tenant (the operator of the building). There is invariably a very direct relationship between the amount of rent charged for business premises and the pedestrian or traffic count — the higher the count, the higher the rent.

However, a low-rent location can sometimes be overcome by spending more on advertising. But if the amount spent on advertising is greater than the rent savings, there is obviously no net benefit in choosing that location.

Sample #1, Offer to Lease, is a rental contract used by a rental agent for a specific landlord. This contract covers many of the topics discussed in this chapter concerning leasing premises for a restaurant.

1. Bare leases

When checking out premises for possible rent, do more than look at the space and determine how large the square foot area is. Check to see if the walls, floor, and ceiling are finished; if not, find out who pays to put the premises in rentable condition.

Some premises, even in shopping centers, are rented as bare leases. Premises rented this way are referred to as a "shell." Generally the utilities are brought only to the walls (stubbed in). You pay for all inside finishing including the kitchen and dining areas, even down to light fixtures, plumbing, window coverings, and heating and air-conditioning equipment. Determine in advance what this is going to cost so there are no unhappy surprises later.

It is normal that any special inside finishing is your responsibility. However, if you are going to do extensive internal remodeling that will subsequently benefit the landlord when your lease expires, see if you can negotiate a reduced rent.

2. Lease agreements

There is no standard form of commercial lease agreement. Each lease agreement must be prepared by the lawyers of the two parties involved depending on the particular circumstances.

SAMPLE #1
OFFER TO LEASE

Ezy Realty Corporation
#106 — 1795 Renter Row
Anytown

Dear _____,

Re: *Rental of premises for restaurant purposes*
from Land & Lord Ltd.

We, *Classic Cuisine Corp.,* having a registered office at *1855 Gourmet Street, Anytown,* hereby offer to lease as Tenant from *Land & Lord Ltd., Anytown,* as Landlord, a portion of the building, having civic address *1234 Leaser Avenue, Anytown,* on the following terms and conditions.

AREA

The premises to be leased to contain approximately thirteen hundred and forty-five (1,345) square feet of rentable space. The measurement of the rentable space to be in accordance with the accepted building measurement standards for the Building Owners and Management Association for similar use of space.

LOCATION

The premises as described under "Area" above are located on the main floor retail area of the building, having civic address *1234 Leaser Avenue, Anytown,* and as delineated in red on the plan attached and marked as "Schedule 1."

RENT

The rent will be $36,000 per annum triple net for the first five (5) years of the lease term. The annual rent for years 6 through 10 inclusive, the Review Period, shall be as mutually agreed between the Landlord and the Tenant not less than six (6) months prior to the expiration of the fifth year of the lease term and the rent shall be based on the then current rental rates prevailing in the immediate area for similar quality and quantity of space and use. In the event that the Landlord and Tenant cannot agree on the rent for the Review Period, the rent shall be determined by arbitration in accordance with the Arbitration Act.

The Tenant shall be responsible for his proportionate share of taxes and operating costs attributable to the premises as described herein.

LEASE TERM

The Lease term shall be for a period of five (5) years and shall commence on *January 1st, 199-.*

OPTION TO RENEW

The Tenant shall have the option to renew the Lease of the premises for a further period of five (5) years, the Renewal Lease. Such option must be exercised in accordance with the terms and conditions of the Landlord's Lease, a copy of which is attached hereto. The amount of the rent for the Renewal Lease shall be as mutually agreed between the Landlord and the Tenant and shall be based on the then current rates prevailing in the immediate area for similar quality and quantity of space and use. In the event that the Landlord and Tenant cannot agree on the rent for the Renewal Lease, the rent shall be determined by arbitration.

USE

It is intended that the premises shall be used for the purpose of a restaurant for the preparing and serving of hot and cold sandwiches, soups, beverages and salad bar, generally but not being limited to a self-service restaurant.

OTHER CONDITIONS

1. The Landlord must provide a Lease in registerable form and the Tenant reserves the right to register the Lease at his sole option.

2. The Tenant reserves the right to sublet or assign the Lease and the Renewal Lease with the Landlord's consent and the Landlord shall not unreasonably withhold his consent to sublet or assign the Lease.

3. The Landlord is to provide the Tenant with flooring, ceiling, and lighting allowance of $10 per square foot.

4. The Tenant is to be permitted to erect such signage as is reasonably required for identification of the restaurant. The construction and erection of the signage shall be solely at the Tenant's expense and the location of the signage shall be as mutually agreed on between the Landlord and the Tenant and shall conform to the Municipal signage criteria.

5. The Landlord is to grant to the Tenant a two (2) months' rent and operating expense abatement from the commencement date of the Lease.

6. The Tenant shall be responsible for securing all necessary building permits and approvals required by the City of *Anytown* for all Tenant leasehold improvements. Such permits will be secured and copies provided to the Landlord prior to the commencement of work on the leasehold improvement.

7. The Tenant does not require venting and makeup air units normally required for a full service restaurant due to the Tenant's menu.

8. If an inordinate amount of garbage is generated by the restaurant, the Landlord can levy a proportional charge.

9. The Landlord's work to be as follows:

   Floors — concrete, smooth ready for finish

   Walls — demising walls primed ready for finish

   Air-conditioning, heating, and venting — supplied except for concealing

   Washrooms — Landlord to provide roughed-in plumbing for three washrooms

   Floor loading — slab is designed to accommodate 100 lbs. per sq. ft. live load

   Electrical — 3 phase 120/208 electrical service with 150 amp. capacity — any metering devices to be the responsibility of the Landlord

   Entrance and exit — Landlord to provide one entrance and one exit

LEASE DOCUMENTATION

If this Offer to Lease is accepted on or prior to the date of acceptance as set out hereinafter, we are prepared to enter into a standard form of Lease prepared by the Landlord, copies of which are attached.

It is the intent that the articles of this Offer to Lease will be incorporated into the Landlord's standard Lease, a copy of which is attached hereto. In the event that this Offer is accepted, the Tenant agrees to enter into and sign the Landlord's standard Lease, as attached and marked as "Schedule 2."

SUBJECTS

This Offer is subject to:

1. The Tenant obtaining the necessary permits and licenses for occupation and use of the premises from all the applicable regulatory authorities.

2. The review, acceptance, and approval by the Tenant's solicitor of the Landlord's Lease as attached.

The subjects as stated herein are for the sole benefit of the Tenant and must be removed in writing by the Tenant by not later than 21 calendar days after acceptance of this Offer to Lease. In the event that the subjects are not removed within the 21 days, this Offer is null and void and there will be no further financial or legal obligation to the Tenant, and the deposit as stated hereinafter is to be returned to *Classic Cuisine Corp.* forthwith without deduction.

DEPOSIT

A deposit of *$5,000* is to be paid prior to removal of the subjects to Ezy Realty Corporation in trust, if this Offer is accepted. If this Offer is not accepted, the deposit is to be returned to *Classic Cuisine Corp.* forthwith without deduction.

COMMISSION

The Landlord will pay Ezy Realty Corp. $3,000 as real estate commission upon signing of the Lease.

ACCEPTANCE

This Offer shall be irrevocable and open for acceptance for a period of five (5) days after the date hereof, expiring at *12:00 noon* on *November 30, 199-*, after which time, if not accepted, it shall be null and void.

DATED at *Anytown* this *25th* day of *November, 199-*.

CLASSIC CUISINE CORP.

per_____
$\qquad\qquad\qquad\qquad\qquad\qquad\qquad$ President

We hereby accept this Offer and agree to be bound by the terms and conditions hereof.

DATED at *Anytown* this *27th* day of *November, 199-*.

per_____
$\qquad\qquad\qquad\qquad\qquad\qquad\qquad$ Director

The agreement should cover such matters as the length of the contract (for example, 5, 10, or even 20 or more years), the amount of rent and frequency of payment, the responsibility of the two parties for the maintenance of the property, and who pays which costs for items such as major (plumbing, electrical, air-conditioning) or minor (cleaning and cleaning supplies) maintenance, and other items of cost such as building alterations, property taxes, and insurance.

Because of the ever-escalating cost of land and property development, property taxes, maintenance, and upgrading, a landlord will try to make rental periods as short as possible to ensure that rental rates high enough to cover all his or her costs can be negotiated more frequently. Your objective is, of course, just the reverse. From your perspective an initial lease of 15 years with two 5-year renewal options would be desirable but may not be achievable without difficult negotiations. A long initial lease period allows you to spread your investment costs over more years.

3. Expense pass-throughs

Some lease contracts contain expense pass-throughs. In other words, some of the landlord's "normal" expenses are now the responsibility of the tenant. The most common pass-through is known as a triple net lease in which the tenant pays for all maintenance, property taxes, and building insurance. This can have a double effect. Any remodeling you do (such as building improvements) increases the value of the building and will thus increase your property taxes, even though you don't own the building!

Similarly, businesses in the area may be assessed a special property tax for improved community lighting, sewers, or other works. As a tenant under triple net you will pay that added burden.

Read the contract carefully, and have your lawyer go over it since some leases state that if you attach anything to floors, walls, or ceilings it becomes the property of the lessor. This means that you could invest several thousand dollars in shelving, special lighting, equipment fixed to the floor, and so on, and as soon as it is installed it is no longer legally yours.

4. Restrictions

Check the contract carefully to see if there are any restrictions on your business operations by the landlord or others, such as any conditions or restrictions on subletting which you may want to do if the restaurant is not successful and your lease still has some time to run. The landlord should not have the right to unreasonably withhold your right to sublet, assign, or mortgage your lease, or even sell it for its remaining life, including options (see below) to someone else. If your restaurant is successful, the right to sell its goodwill for a profit can be quite valuable to you.

Measure your floor space so that, if rent is based on square foot area, you will not be charged for more space than you have. However, note that in some shopping malls "your" space includes a share of common areas such as halls, storage areas, elevators, and similar areas. Find out in advance what your share of this common space is.

5. Renewal option

An initial relatively short contract with one or more renewal options is often preferable to a long-term lease contract. Renewal options prevent you from being locked in if the business is not successful, but allow you to continue if it is a profitable enterprise. Any renewal options and their terms should be written into the initial contract.

In older buildings in a city core, landlords may be very reluctant to include options since they never know when an offer may come along from an investor wishing to tear down the building and construct a new one. Your successful restaurant with two or three renewals could be an obstacle for the landlord.

With reference to a renewal option, note that any change in rent rates should be negotiated for the new period near the end of the present lease term. If you have the right to a renewal term, it is important to give the landlord a renewal notice within the time frame stipulated in the contract otherwise you might find that you lose your right to a renewal option.

6. Fixtures and equipment

The typical lease is generally only for the land and building, with the lessee (operator) purchasing and owning the fixtures and equipment. If the equipment and similar items are owned by the lessor (in which case the lease payments will generally be higher), the lease agreement should specify how frequently these items are to be replaced and at whose cost. If you own the equipment and similar items, the lease contract should provide for the disposition of them at the end of the lease period. The two most common arrangements are that you are responsible for complete removal of such items at your cost, or that the lessor has the right to buy them at some stipulated value.

7. Contingencies

Make sure any necessary contingencies are in the contract. Contingencies might be that the contract depends on your request for a liquor license being approved, or that financing for equipment purchasing is obtained, or that all necessary government licenses, permits, and variances are approved. Finally, a contingency that you may inspect the site to check that it conforms to the lease description should be included.

b. RENTAL ARRANGEMENTS

With any form of lease operation, it is normal for you to bear the burden of any operating losses, although, depending on the lease arrangement, some of the net profit may have to be shared with the lessor under certain circumstances.

A variety of rental arrangements are possible with leasing. Some of them are discussed here.

1. Fixed rental

A fixed rental arrangement calls for straight payments during the term of the lease. The payment might be a stepped one that increases, for example, year by year during the term of the lease. However, the payments are not variable with, and do not depend on, your sales or profits.

The lease agreement will probably allow renegotiation of the fixed amount of rent during the life of the agreement, particularly if the life is for an extended number of years.

If a fixed rental cost appears cheap when based on a dollar amount per square foot of leased space, do not be misled if it appears to be lower than the market rates. In other words, make sure that there are no "hidden" expenses.

2. Variable rental

A variable rental has a fixed portion, usually at least sufficient to give the lessor cash flow to amortize loan obligations, cover expenses, and provide a return on investment. As well, there will be additional rent based either on your gross sales or on your net profit.

The variable rent portion gives the landlord some hedge against inflation, although there might be a ceiling rent amount stated in the contract.

3. Percentage of sales

Another possibility is for rent to be based on sales. If this is so, what is to be included in sales should be completely spelled out. For example, is rental income from a cigarette vending machine in your restaurant waiting area to be included in sales?

Most contracts allow for a declining percentage as sales increase. For example, rent may be 6% of sales up to a certain level, then decline to 5% for any sales above that level.

Some contracts call for an increasing percentage of sales, or an escalation clause. This can be risky for you since the accelerating percentage can seriously erode normal net profit margins as sales continue to climb.

4. Percentage of profit

With rent partly based on percentage of sales, the landlord is in a kind of partnership arrangement with you. With the variable portion of rent based on profit, this partnership becomes even more firm. The profit must be carefully defined in the lease contract as either profit before income tax, profit before interest and tax, or profit before depreciation, interest, and tax.

5. Other considerations

Note that rental terms quoted by a landlord are negotiable, even if the landlord tries to make you believe otherwise. For example, if the landlord wants you as a tenant you may be able to negotiate that the landlord provide all improvements to meet the occupancy code for use of that space by a restaurant and provide the required electrical, heating, ventilation, and air conditioning systems. Even at this early stage you should have a design firm specializing in restaurant facilities (or a food facilities consultant) involved in the process because they can provide appropriate advice about power and other needed services.

Many landlords will stipulate that you must use architects and/or designers in any remodeling of premises. Their cost can be very surprising.

Before signing any lease make sure you have all area bylaw and zoning clearances and preferably include in the lease a release clause protecting you against restrictions prohibiting your type of operation or affecting important operating practices. For example, if you plan to serve alcoholic beverages, will licensing authorities permit it in that location? Also, confirm that "shell" packages have the necessary factors for restaurant use: fire-rated walls, sprinklers, appropriate entrance and exit doors, plumbing, and electrical services.

In some lease contracts, to protect the landlord, the amount of certain types of expenses may be limited. For example, if your salary is not limited you could pay yourself such an inflated amount that there would be no profit to be shared with the landlord in the rent.

In other cases, the contract may specify a minimum expense amount that you must spend each year, for example, for advertising so that sufficient sales and profit are generated, or for maintenance so that the building is kept in good condition.

Use the checklist in Worksheet #1 to create a profile of any space you might rent.

c. SALE/LEASEBACK

One other type of lease arrangement is the sale/leaseback. This occurs when a building owner sells the land to a land investor and agrees to lease it back for a number of years.

Alternatively, the owner may sell both land and the building to a property investor and contract to lease both of them back in order to be able to continue to operate the business.

If you are unable to obtain a lease on ideal premises because the owner wishes to sell, it may be advisable to seek a sale/leaseback arrangement. You might be able to arrange in advance with a third party that, at the time of the purchase, these assets will be immediately sold to that third party under a leaseback arrangement to you.

WORKSHEET #1
PROFILE OF RENTAL SPACE

❑ How long is the lease contract term?

❑ What renewal options are there?

❑ What is the rental cost per square foot and exactly how many square feet are there?

❑ What is the percentage rent if based on sales?

❑ What are the common area expenses?

❑ Is any up-front security deposit required?

❑ If you, as tenant, pay property taxes, how much are they?

❑ If you, as tenant, pay building insurance, how much is it?

❑ If you, as tenant, pay building maintenance, how much is it?

❑ What is the cost of utilities?

❑ Does the landlord provide any cash allowance for leasehold improvements to put the building into rentable condition? If so, does this have to be refunded or is the rental cost increased in order to pay for this allowance?

❑ Are there any menu restrictions?

❑ Are there any interior design restrictions imposed either by local authorities or by the landlord?

❑ Are there any signage restrictions either by local authorities or by the landlord?

❑ What other landlord restrictions are there?

❑ What are the landlord's rights?

❑ What are your rights?

❑ What personal covenants might the lease contract contain?

WORKSHEET #1 — Continued

Use the following checklist to determine if the leased premises are suitable for your operation's needs from a physical point of view and to determine the cost of making them suitable if any upgrading is required.

Item	Suitable	Inadequate	Estimated cost
Electrical supply			
Plumbing supply			
Gas supply			
Oil supply			
Lighting system			
Ventilation system			
Air-conditioning system			
Sprinkler system			
Fire-rated walls			
Handicapped access			
Handicapped facilities			
Employee facilities			
Customer reception area			
Dining area seating			
Food preparation space			
Food pick-up space			
Dishwashing area space			
Office space			
Delivery truck access			
Receiving area space			
Receiving area security			
Food storage space			
Liquor storage space			
Inventory security			
Cleaning supplies space			
Garbage container space			
Garbage removal access			
Customer parking			
Other items:			

Under some sale/leaseback arrangements, you may also be able to structure the contract so that, at the end of the lease period, you regain ownership of the building and/or land.

d. ADVANTAGES OF LEASING

Some advantages of leasing are:

(a) Under a lease arrangement you have the obvious advantage of not having to provide capital to buy the property. Any capital that you might have is then available for investment elsewhere.

(b) Your borrowing power is freed up to raise money, if required, for more critical areas of the business.

(c) Lease payments on a building are generally fully tax deductible.

(d) Owned land is not depreciable for tax purposes, but the cost of leasing land is tax deductible.

(e) Any leasehold improvements that you make to the building are generally amortized over the life of the lease rather than over the life of the building. The lease period is normally less than the building life therefore providing a tax saving.

(f) You may have a purchase option at the end of the lease period when it may be desirable to buy and cash is available to do so.

(g) If and when the time comes to sell the business, it may be easier to do this if there is no real estate involved.

(h) Although you would not normally have this in mind when entering a lease transaction, in case of unexpected bankruptcy, you would probably only be liable for one year's rent rather than long-term mortgage payments on a property you purchased.

(i) Finally, it may be possible to arrange a lease with rental payments adjusted to the restaurant's seasonal cash flows, even though total annual rent would be the same amount.

e. DISADVANTAGES OF LEASING

Some disadvantages of leasing are:

(a) In a lease arrangement, any capital gain in the assets accrues to the landlord and not to you. In a similar way, at the expiry of the lease, the value of the future profit of the business that you have worked hard to build up does not benefit you unless the lease is renewed.

(b) The cost of a lease may be higher than some other form of financing.

(c) It may also be more difficult for you to borrow money with leased premises if there are no assets (other than a lease agreement) to pledge as collateral.

(d) Finally, the total cash outflow in rental payments may be greater in the long run than for purchasing the property.

f. RENTAL AGENTS

If you are negotiating a lease through a rental agent, remember that that agent has only one mandate: to rent empty space for the landlord as quickly as possible to earn a commission. You know, or should know, more about what you want for your particular restaurant than the agent. In other words, be prepared by arming yourself in advance with as many facts as possible about the type and particularly the size of premises you need.

Also, be alert to agents whose main motivation is to rent you less than adequate premises, particularly in a poor location for your type of restaurant.

g. EQUIPMENT LEASE

Consider also the possibility of leasing any needed fixtures and equipment in order to lower your startup costs. Some sites, if they were previously occupied by a restaurant, may come already equipped with usable equipment and furnishings. In other cases, if the premises are a shell, you will have to find your own equipment and furnishings. Some equipment suppliers will lease directly. In other cases, you will lease from a company that specializes in leasing and has bought the equipment from the supplier. The supplier may act as an intermediary in such cases.

Most equipment leases cannot be canceled and require you to make a series of payments whose total sum will exceed the cost of assets if purchased outright, since the lessor has to make a profit on his or her investment. Depreciation of the assets is the lessor's prerogative as owner of the assets. Maintenance is usually, but not invariably, a cost of the lessor.

Generally, the lessor owns any residual value in the assets, although contracts sometimes give you the option to purchase the assets at a specified price at the end of the lease period. In such cases, the lease purchase is actually a type of conditional sale and you would have any tax advantages that claiming expenses such as depreciation may offer.

In some cases, you will also have the option to renew the lease for a specified further period.

1. Advantages of equipment leasing

There are some advantages to leasing equipment. Flexibility is considered to be an advantage because you avoid the risk of obsolescence you might otherwise have if the assets are purchased outright. However, the lessor probably considers the cost of obsolescence when the lease rates are determined.

You also avoid the problems of maintenance and its cost. However, the lessor will normally build the cost of maintenance into the lease payments. If there is no down payment required, 100% financing of leased assets may be possible. For relatively short-lived assets like equipment and fixtures, this is an advantage even if you have the cash to pay for them outright. This cash is then free for investment in longer-lived assets like land and buildings that frequently appreciate as time goes by. Equipment depreciates very rapidly and usually has little or no residual value.

Finally, income tax is an important consideration. Since lease payments are generally fully tax deductible, there can be an advantage in leasing. On the other hand, ownership permits deduction for income tax purposes of both depreciation and the interest expense on any debt financing of the purchase. However, what might be advantageous with one lease arrangement may be disadvantageous with another. Each situation must be considered on its own merits as far as tax implications are concerned.

A sale/leaseback of equipment is also not uncommon. You simply sell your equipment to a bank, finance company, or even a leasing firm at a price close to its current market value and then lease it back for its remaining usable life. However, the lease costs may be comparatively high since the lessor receives little or no tax benefit (for example, through depreciation) for owning used equipment. In addition, there may be sales or use taxes on the transaction.

2. Disadvantages of equipment leasing

One disadvantage of leasing equipment is that money borrowed to make the lease payments can be more expensive (by an interest point or more) than money borrowed to purchase the equipment outright.

Also, the lessor is the owner of the equipment and has the right to repossess it if you do not meet payments. If you owned the equipment, you would not lose any residual value remaining in the equipment.

h. ARCHITECT AND CONTRACTOR

If the improvements to your leased premises are major you will have to hire an architect at an early stage in order to determine the cost of improvements since that cost can influence your decision about whether or not to sign a lease. The architect's services will later have to be supplemented by those of a contractor. If modifications to the premises are minor, then you can probably bypass an architect and deal only with a contractor.

1. Leasehold improvement costs

You can obtain a rough idea of what leasehold improvement costs will be by estimating the cost per square foot. For example, the cost of preparing plans, obtaining necessary permits, making all utility connections to the landlord's existing ones, building partitions, finishing all ceilings, floors, and walls, will be in the area of $200 to $250 per square foot of leased space.

To this must be added the cost of equipment and furnishings which will vary considerably depending on such matters as your menu, the restaurant's size, and the quality of furnishings desired. For example, the total cost for a 1,000 square foot restaurant could range anywhere from $50,000 to $200,000.

If you are taking over an existing restaurant where only limited leasehold improvements are required, the costs might range from $50 to $150 per square foot. Cost of equipment and furnishings in this situation will depend on how much of the existing equipment and furniture you can use and how much must be replaced.

To leasehold improvement and equipment costs you must add dining area furniture and tableware (china, glass, silverware) costs. A useful rule of thumb is to use a per seat figure. For a restaurant other than a fast food one using primarily disposables, this will generally range from $200 to $250 per seat.

2. Preliminary work

If you need to employ an architect, his or her time (and thus costs) can be minimized if you do a lot of preliminary work (perhaps in discussion with a consultant) about the restaurant's budget, design, layout, and initial plans.

For example, how many seats do you want and can you place in the dining area? Generally, a minimum of 12 square feet per person is required but it is possible to increase seating capacity by changing table sizes. What seating configuration (counters, tables for two, four, or six, and booths) is most appropriate for your proposed clientele? For example, if you have 100 seats available with tables capable of accommodating groups of four, and you expect to be serving some couples, you will have to assign tables of four to only two people. If you purchase a proportion of tables for two, this will allow you to seat more people at any one time, thus increasing your sales and profits. If necessary, tables for two can be joined together to handle larger groups.

If you can provide the architect with prints of the existing building plans this will also speed up the process and reduce architectural costs because existing blueprints will show present utility outlet locations and the architect can work around them to minimize remodeling work.

3. Decision to proceed

With a knowledge of local codes and regulations, the architect will then advise you whether or not your ideas are feasible. If your ideas are feasible, he or she can then provide sketches and a detailed cost estimate. With approval of these matters, you can advise the architect to proceed. If cost estimates are higher than your budget, you and the architect can agree on changes that can be made to reduce costs.

Once the decision to proceed is made, the architect will draw up more detailed plans showing such things as location of columns, walls, partitions, and dimensions, along with specifications for materials, furniture, and equipment.

With plans and specifications, appropriate approvals (such as for building, health, zoning, and fire) can then be obtained from appropriate government authorities and potential contractors and furniture and equipment suppliers will also have the information they need to make bids. You and the architect can review these bids, decide which one(s) to accept, and construction can begin.

4. Other startup costs

Don't forget to add to the architect's figures an amount for other startup costs such as the following:

- Legal and accounting fees
- Consulting fees
- Menu printing
- Uniforms
- Initial inventory purchase
- Preopening salaries and wages

- Preopening advertising
- Deposits for utilities and telephone
- Preopening insurance
- Prepaid rent
- Working capital

It is difficult to put a dollar figure on these startup costs because they will differ so widely depending on the type and size of restaurant.

i. FURTHER READING

If you are interested in learning about restaurant design, the following books are recommended:

(a) *Food Service Planning: Layout and Equipment* by Lendal H. Kotschevar and Margaret E. Terrell. (New York: John Wiley, 1977).

(b) *Successful Restaurant Design* by Regina S. Baraban and Joseph F. Durocher. (New York: Van Nostrand Reinhold, 1989).

(c) *Design and Layout of Foodservice Facilities* by John Birchfield. (New York: Van Nostrand Reinhold, 1988).

7
BUILDING CONSTRUCTION

If you plan to rent the premises for your restaurant, you might wish to skip over most of this chapter concerning building construction. However, there are some items in the section on "Pre-opening schedule" that apply equally to opening a business in leased premises.

If you construct a building, some detailed costing will be required so that your financial plan (see chapter 10) can be more accurately prepared.

As mentioned in the last chapter, you probably shouldn't be thinking about constructing your own building when you first start out in your new restaurant venture. The risk of failure is increased because of the increased capital needed. However, there may be exceptions. For example, to establish a franchised business, the franchisor may insist that you own a free-standing building. In such situations, the franchisor ought to be able to provide the financing, or help in finding financing.

a. CONSTRUCTION COST

If the land has to be purchased prior to building construction, the cost of this land should be known, although to it must be added any costs involved in preparing the site for construction, and possibly even landscaping costs.

Parking space is also a consideration. On average, including entrance and driveway areas, you may need 250 to 300 square feet per car. A rough rule of thumb is $3 to $4 per square foot for land preparation for landscaping and/or parking.

1. Size of building

The type of restaurant you want will influence its size. A commercial family restaurant is usually larger than a gourmet one, while a deli or fast food restaurant will be relatively small since it may have no tables or chairs. However, for any particular kind of restaurant your investment budget can also dictate the size of building you can afford.

As a rough rule of thumb, for seating area a coffee shop will require 10 to 12 square feet per seat and a dining room 14 to 16 square feet per seat. A gourmet restaurant could require as much as 20 to 30 square feet. To this must be added food receiving, storage, and processing space plus washrooms, waiting areas, and office(s). This could be as little as 20% of total space requirement, or as much as 50%.

2. Cost of building

The cost of constructing the building must be estimated. One of the most useful methods of estimating cost is based on the cost of construction per square foot for that type of building in that locality.

The square foot requirements for total space are simply multiplied by the current cost per square foot. The total cost may have to be adjusted upward for special features of the building that might increase its basic construction cost — for example, the cost of an elevator if the building is two or more stories tall. If a more detailed costing is desired for land and building, use Worksheet #2 to break down costs.

WORKSHEET #2
BREAKDOWN OF SITE AND BUILDING COSTS

GENERAL:
Permits, plans, surveys $_____
Fees $_____

SITE:
Land purchase $_____

SITE WORK:
Clearing $_____
Services: Wiring $_____
   Sewer $_____
   Water $_____
Excavation $_____
Fill $_____
Paving and/or gravel $_____
Landscaping $_____
Fencing $_____
Labor $_____

CONCRETE:
Footings $_____
Foundations $_____
Reinforcing $_____
Floors $_____
Labor $_____

WALLS:
Concrete blocks $_____
Masonry $_____
Woodwork $_____
Partitions $_____
Drywall $_____
Sheeting $_____
Insulation $_____
Labor $_____

WALL OPENINGS:
Doors $_____
Windows $_____
Ventilation $_____
Labor $_____

CARRIED FORWARD $_____

BROUGHT FORWARD $_____

ROOF:
Materials $_____
Labor $_____

FINISHES:
Millwork $_____
Floors $_____
Ceilings $_____
Furnishings $_____
Labor $_____

ELECTRICAL:
Wiring $_____
Fixtures $_____
Other $_____
Labor $_____

PLUMBING:
Materials $_____
Labor $_____

HEATING:
Materials $_____
Labor $_____

PAINTING:
Materials $_____
Labor $_____

HARDWARE:
Materials $_____
Labor $_____

OTHER ITEMS:
Air-conditioning $_____
Elevators $_____
Sprinkler $_____
Sign $_____

TOTAL COST $_____

3. Total costs

To the land and building cost, you must then add the cost of other items, including equipment and furniture (discussed in more detail in the next chapter) to arrive at total cost. When the total estimated cost of the site and building has been calculated, add your estimate of architect and other consultants' fees, plus a reserve for contingencies of, let us say, 10% to 20%.

This contingency is necessary to take care of actual costs that exceed estimates, of extras that are not anticipated, and building changes that are not perceived until the building is well underway.

You will probably find that your total cost will be in the range of $50 to $100 per square foot. In other words, if you need a 10,000 square foot land and building area, its cost, with equipment and furnishings, will be somewhere between $500,000 and $1,000,000.

A typical breakdown for a sit-down restaurant might be as follows:

Legal, architect, fees, permits	$ 30,000
Land and site preparation	150,000
Building construction (frame and/or brick)	230,000
Kitchen equipment and furnishings	90,000
Contingency	50,000
TOTAL	$550,000

To pay for this kind of investment, you need projected sales of at least $500,000 annually. In fact, a general rule of thumb for any type of restaurant, regardless of size, is that for each $1 invested you must achieve $1 of sales for it to be profitable.

4. Architects and designers

When you are constructing your own building on a selected site you will need to employ an architect and possibly an interior designer if the architect does not have one on staff.

The process of preparing preliminary and final plans is similar to that outlined in chapter 6 for leasehold improvements except that the detail is more involved, time required longer, and cost considerably higher.

b. CHOICE OF CONSTRUCTION APPROACH

When you have design plans prepared and specifications approved by local authorities, you must then choose the method to use for construction coordination. You can employ a general contractor, a project supervisor, or a manager, or supervise the job yourself.

Regardless of which method is selected, responsibility for supervision of the contractor's work should be left to the architect and the consultants who may have been employed. This will ensure that building construction is carried out within the terms and conditions of the contract.

The many diverse techniques and variety of types of contracts should be discussed with the architect, who is familiar with them. This discussion should take place at an early stage in the development of the working drawings since any subsequent changes can considerably affect the construction time schedule and cost.

1. Employ a general contractor

A common method of construction is to employ a general contractor. Contractors would be required to submit bids or tenders on the entire building construction after they have had an opportunity to review the building specifications. These tenders can be open to all contractors or be closed or limited to those contractors who are known for their high quality construction standards. The contractor's price includes labor, material, and supervisory costs, plus the contractor's own profit.

When a contractor puts in a bid, costs should be detailed. The contractor's fee is usually about 10% of the total building cost. For this the contractor obtains all permits, supervises and pays for all tradespeople, purchases and pays for all materials used (including shipping charges), coordinates all the various subcontractors, and guarantees the finished building.

There should be no "extras" unless they have been agreed to. This might occur if the contractor is unable to obtain a price at the time the bid is made. In such cases, some protection against exorbitant costs for that possibility should be built into the contract.

Also, there is the possibility that you might change some item of design during construction, which could change the final construction costs.

2. Employ a project supervisor

An alternative to hiring a general contractor is to have a project supervisor or manager negotiate with you and your architect for the construction of the project.

In such a case, the project supervisor will be responsible for tendering and hiring of the subtrades, and then supervising them. You are responsible for purchasing all construction materials and paying the tradespeople involved, and the project supervisor or manager simply receives a fee for the supervisory responsibilities.

One advantage of this method is that the architect may issue certain drawings in sequence, permitting an early start on construction before total completion of all working drawings and specifications.

With this approach, you must be careful to establish a maximum allowable building construction cost. The project supervisor, or better still the architect or you, should use the services of a qualified surveyor or building estimator to establish the probable maximum total building construction cost and to ensure a system of continuing cost control.

3. Owner supervision of construction

Another alternative to construction approach is for you to supervise the construction. This will eliminate the profit of the general contractor, or the fee of the project supervisor, but add considerably to the demands on your time. Unless you have considerable experience in construction this route is not recommended.

If you do handle the construction yourself, you should write down the estimated costs. A useful form for this is illustrated in Worksheet #2. Complete this form before construction starts to obtain a relatively firm idea of what is involved in total outlay for construction.

4. Risks in contracting

Avoid any "cost plus" contract where the contractor agrees to do the work on the basis of cost of all labor, material, and subcontracting costs, plus a percentage of those total costs as contractor profit.

Given this leeway, a contractor can pad or kite invoices, present invoices that have already been paid from another job, pad hours of labor actually paid for, or even have "ghost" employees on the payroll. In addition, the contractor's subcontractors could submit fraudulent invoices, with the contractor and subcontractor splitting the extra profits. You would have to have some in-depth experience in contracting to know these things were happening.

Another risk is that, in many jurisdictions, a contractor can place a lien on your building if you fail to pay. This is reasonable; however, even if you pay in full and the contractor fails to pay the subcontractors, suppliers, or employees, then those people can also put a lien on your property!

Control over a contractor is achieved through bonding. Two types of bond are common. A bid bond means that the contractor guarantees that construction will start when specified in the tender. A performance bond provides you with funds to complete the building if the contractor runs into difficulties and cannot complete the contract or does not make payments to others that should be made. The cost of bonds can run from 1% to 5% of the gross contract amount.

The construction contract can also include penalty clauses such as one that requires the contractor to pay you a specified sum of money if construction is incomplete by a stated date. Contracts with construction companies should always be reviewed by your lawyer before they are signed.

c. CONTRACT DETAILS

Regardless of which method of construction supervision you use, a formal contract should be drawn up. Apart from defining the legal implications of the contract, such as stating the names of the supervisory architect, building owner, and contractor, the contract should spell out at least the following contractor responsibilities:

(a) Supervision and construction procedures

(b) Cost control of labor and materials

(c) Warranty responsibilities for permits, fees, notices, taxes, and cash allowances

(d) Responsibility of work superintendent and other employees

(e) Preparation of progress schedules

(f) Maintenance on the building site of drawings and specifications that will be available to you

(g) Channels for communication

(h) Site cleanup

(i) Procedures for claims for damages

(j) Your rights upon default of the contractor

(k) Contract fee payment amounts and methods, including circumstances warranting withholdings for non-performance

(l) Final payment for work completion

(m) Construction insurance requirements and responsibilities

(n) Contract termination by either party

(o) Bonding requirements

(p) Penalty clauses

This is only a "bare bones" list to indicate some of the important considerations to be included in a construction contract. It is not intended to be all-inclusive, but only to point out some of the many considerations involved in construction of a new building.

Consultation with a lawyer is imperative when drawing up construction contracts.

d. INSURANCE

An important consideration during construction is to protect money that is invested in the building as it is constructed. This protection is handled by insurance.

Indeed, before construction even begins, you would be wise to study the many comprehensive multiple line protection policies offered by the insurance companies that are competitive in the field.

The basic type of insurance coverage required is for loss to buildings and personal property on a stipulated peril basis (such as fire, lightning, and earthquake). In addition, consider optional coverage for sprinkler leakage, vandalism, malicious mischief, and public liability.

Generally, building insurance covers all permanent fixtures (including items such as heating, cooling, air-conditioning, elevators, and similar engineering and/or mechanical equipment) as well as signs attached to the building.

As building construction progresses, the insurance policy should provide for periodic automatic increases in the building insurance amount.

e. PRE-OPENING SCHEDULE

Since the construction time for any particular building can vary because of such factors as size and type of construction, the following can only be a rough guide to the steps involved and their timing prior to opening.

1. One to two years before opening

During this period, preliminary architectural drawings should be completed and local planning authorities contacted to ensure that design and construction practices do not violate basic planning guidelines and regulatory requirements. In addition, electrical and mechanical engineers should be engaged to provide the design of, or design advice on, such items as electrical systems, heating and plumbing, air-conditioning, and possibly elevators.

2. One to one and one-half years before opening

Search and application for financing the building must begin. Construction tenders should be called for (this usually takes about a month). If interior designers and landscape architects are to be used, their services should be contracted for during this period when the final design work for the building should also be completed.

This final design should be approved by all necessary local government agencies or authorities so that a building permit can be applied for. If an interior designer is to be used, he or she should produce final drawings and specifications for fixtures, furniture, and equipment so that tenders can be called.

3. One year before opening

About one year before opening, construction should be well on the way, or at least have been started. An office should be set up on the site with a telephone. A mailing address with the restaurant's name should be established with the post office.

Pre-opening expenses must be estimated to ensure that funds will be available to pay for them.

4. Six months before opening

Product prices should be established. The opening date should be fairly definitely set, and any advertising campaign planned (radio, newspapers, and any other media).

5. Three to six months before opening

Begin the search for key employees (such as the chef and/or dining room manager) to be hired. If service contracts are to be arranged for any necessary equipment, they should be signed.

6. One month before opening

By now the opening date should be set. Key employees should have been hired and final decision made on which applicants for jobs are to be hired. Key employees should supervise the installation of fixtures and equipment. They should have prepared lists of necessary operating supplies so that these can be ordered and delivered prior to opening.

7. One to three weeks before opening

All staff should be on the premises for training and orientation. Dry runs should be carried out on inventory location, equipment use, and food and beverage preparation, pick-up, and service procedures. These dry runs will help test all the facilities. If there are any problems with equipment not working properly or similar matters, they can be detected and corrected before the first customers arrive to be served.

8

EQUIPMENT AND FURNISHINGS

Equipment is a major consideration when starting a restaurant. If you are moving into rented premises that previously housed a restaurant, then most, if not all, of the major equipment items may already be there and their cost will be built into your rent.

Undoubtedly, regardless of the condition of the equipment and furnishings, you will be faced with remodeling costs in premises that previously housed a restaurant. These remodeling costs could run as high as $500 to $750 per seat which, for a 100-seat restaurant, works out as $50,000 to $75,000.

a. COST OF EQUIPMENT

If you need to purchase equipment, the cost can be high. A rule of thumb is that the investment in food preparation and serving equipment is approximately $1,000 per seat, or a total of $100,000 in a 100-seat restaurant. This is only a rule of thumb. A take-out restaurant might be able to cut this cost considerably, whereas a gourmet restaurant might well exceed the $1,000 per seat figure.

The other alternative is to lease your new equipment from a supplier as discussed in chapter 6 on leasing. You might also ask your supply company if they have reconditioned equipment at a lower cost. Alternatively, you could try an auction. With the high mortality rate in the restaurant industry, you will probably find frequent restaurant equipment auctions in most towns and cities. You might be able to obtain good equipment at reasonable prices — but you have to know what you are looking for and its market value.

b. FIT EQUIPMENT TO NEEDS

Since equipment is costly, you must fit the equipment you are going to buy to your specific needs to reduce the investment cost. The major factors that influence equipment requirements are as follows.

1. Menu

Your menu is the most important factor influencing your equipment requirements. For example, a fast food, short-order restaurant may have a griddle and deep fat fryer as an equipment requirement, but would have little or no need for a broiler or roasting oven.

Food preparation methods for your menu items are also a consideration. If you are going to prepare all your foods from scratch, then you are going to need different equipment than if you used a lot of prepared foods. For example, a gourmet restaurant making its own sauces and soups from raw ingredients may need stoves, ranges, and ovens, along with related stockpots, roasting pans, and other cooking equipment that a fast food restaurant would not need.

2. Storage areas

Your menu and food preparation methods can have a dramatic impact on your storage area and storage area equipment requirements. For example, a gourmet restaurant producing all food from raw ingredients may require extensive refrigerated and dry storage areas with their related equipment, whereas a restaurant using primarily convenience food items (such as precooked, prepackaged, and frozen entrées) will require mostly freezer space and freezer equipment.

3. Hours of opening

Hours of opening can affect equipment needs. For example, breakfast service requires the use of a griddle for bacon, egg, and pancake cooking, and possibly such items as omelet pans. A lunch and dinner restaurant may not need these items. A 24-hour restaurant might need considerably more variety in cooking and storage equipment than would a lunch and dinner only operation.

4. Level of service

The type of restaurant you have dictates in part the level of service to be provided, which in turn influences your equipment requirements.

For example, the kitchen equipment requirements for a cafeteria will vary considerably from those of a gourmet restaurant. A cafeteria food service line needs an extensive steam table to display and hold large volumes of food at high temperatures, whereas a gourmet restaurant would not need this type of equipment because much of the food is cooked to order. A gourmet restaurant, on the other hand, may need equipment for flambe work at the table, along with special food service platters. In addition, the furniture and decor will be considerably more expensive in a gourmet restaurant.

5. Budget

Finally, your budget limitations may require that you spend less than would be desirable. In other words, you may have to lower the quality of equipment that you buy.

c. KITCHEN DESIGN AND YOUR MENU

Let's have a look at the way your menu can influence the need for and the positioning of your equipment and the design of your kitchen.

Go over your menu item by item and visualize the flow of materials and people. Where are you going to make salads, prepare sandwiches, cook omelets? List every food ingredient you need and mentally track each one from receiving through storing, issuing, production, and service. Visualize the work flow. For example, suppose you have a simple hamburger on your menu. How much will you buy at a time — a day's supply or a week's? Your delivered hamburger meat must be weighed on a receiving scale or be portion counted if purchased that way.

It must be refrigerated or frozen until needed. Each day's patties must be prepared, or if purchased ready made, they must be defrosted. The patties will have to be stored on trays close to the grill ready for cooking. You need to order buns, probably daily. What about weekends? Where will you store them until used? They should be close to the hamburger cooking area in drawers or airtight containers. Will they be toasted or warmed before use? What equipment is used to do this?

Tomatoes, onions, and any other garnishes must similarly be ordered and stored. What quality, and in what quantity, will you order? Slicing equipment is needed for tomatoes and onions. When will this slicing be done and where?

Potatoes must be ordered in bulk or purchased prepared as french fries to accompany the hamburger. How much should you order at a time? Is there adequate storage space? If purchased in bulk, who cleans, peels, and cuts up the fries? Where is the fryer to be located? What capacity will it have? What quality fat will you use? In what quantities will it be ordered and how stored?

How are hamburger patty, bun, garnish, and french fries put together for serving? Is there adequate working space efficiently arranged for all these items so that they are handy for final preparation?

Where will the final product sit for pick-up by a server or by the customer? Is there space for several orders? Will you need heat lamps to keep orders hot while waiting to be picked up?

These are only some of the questions that you must ask about each of your menu items. You must visualize this process for each menu item and its various ingredients so that you can economize on storage and working space as well as motion by placing related functions together.

Note that there are reputable equipment dealers who specialize in design and layout of kitchens, and furniture suppliers who specialize in dining area layouts, and whose services for doing this are free as long as you purchase necessary equipment from them.

d. EQUIPMENT REQUIREMENTS

1. Kitchen equipment

A major expense is an exhaust hood to remove noxious fumes, odors, and grease-filled air. A proper hood will have automatic fire control systems that should also automatically shut off gas and/or electricity in case of a fire.

Other major items of cooking equipment include the following:

Broiler	Convection oven
Oven	Fryer
Range	Steam kettle
Grill	Microwave oven
Hot top	Salamander or cheese melter

In some cases, some of the items in the above list can be incorporated into one item of equipment. For example, an oven can often be found with combination top burners and a griddle, as well as a broiler or salamander. You should purchase in standard sizes so that, for example, standard size roasting pans will fit into standard width and depth ovens.

There is an endless number of equipment pieces that you could order to use in your new restaurant kitchen. But, of course, money and space will limit your plans for a dream kitchen. As you design your kitchen, keep the following basic items in mind, for present or future purchase.

Chopper	Portion scale
Slicer	Ice machine
Mixer	Dishwasher
Toaster	Sinks
Food warmer	Shelves
Milk dispenser	Pots and pans
Coffee maker	Mixing bowls and whips
Table-mounted can opener	Knives, ladles, and similar items

2. Bar area

If you are selling alcoholic beverages, a storage and bar area with equipment will be required. What drink storage and bar preparation equipment you buy will depend on whether you serve only beer and wine, or beer, wine, and liquor.

Bar supply companies can help you with this since you may have space limitations in such areas as drink display (back bar) and drink preparation. Supply companies can also advise you about types of glassware (both in variety and quantity) to buy to suit your style of restaurant and its decor.

3. Dining area

In your dining area, you must consider the need for the obvious items such as tables and chairs, dining area work stations, and the cash register.

In addition, for each seat in your restaurant you will need at least three sets of each type of plate, bowl, cup, saucer, knife, fork, spoon, and glass. Again, restaurant supply companies can help you select styles of china, glassware, and silverware for your kind of restaurant.

You will also need condiment shakers or holders, water pitchers, ice buckets, trays, ashtrays, teapots, creamers, and similar items. If you want to prepare your own list of smallware, you can visit restaurants similar to your own to see what they are using.

Obviously, if you plan to operate a take-out restaurant, your needs will be quite different since you will be purchasing disposable items.

4. Sales control equipment

An important item of equipment for any restaurant is a sales register. To select sales control equipment for your type of restaurant, you should contact sales equipment suppliers for demonstrations of their systems prior to committing yourself to any particular one. Also, ask for the names of restaurants using each supplier's equipment and talk to those operators about its capabilities, reliability, ease of use, and maintenance problems. There are three major types of equipment:

(a) Electronic cash register

These are relatively cheap registers with limited features that are easy to operate and maintain. A small restaurant would use this type of equipment. Minimum features you need are —

(a) Large keyboard

(b) Large guest check display monitor

(c) Ability to automatically print an item's price on a guest sales check when the menu item or drink key is pressed. This prevents pricing errors.

(d) Automatic tax calculation

(e) Cash receipt dispenser

(b) Sophisticated electronic cash register

This type of equipment would be needed by a large restaurant that needs a register with several hundred price look-ups (PLUs) so that when specific keyboard keys are used the machine is programmed to look up and print on the guest check the item's name and price. This type of equipment is programmable (menu items and menu prices can be changed as frequently as desired), will have a guest check printer, and can have remote printers in kitchen and bar areas. This type of equipment should be able to record both cash and credit sales per server so that totals can be printed out at each shift end. Make sure you buy equipment with a battery to protect the machine's memory in the event of a power failure.

(c) Computerized system

This would only be used by an extremely large restaurant or a chain operation.

e. PROFESSIONAL HELP

The selection of equipment is one area where you should not be shy about seeking professional help. Equipment suppliers will gladly offer advice, particularly if you can be specific about your restaurant type and its menu. These professionals can match the equipment and decor you need to the type of food you are serving and the limitations of your budget.

However, there are salespeople who may try to sell you more equipment than you really need. Therefore, the more knowledgeable you can make yourself beforehand about what you want the better you will be able to deal with that situation.

For example, if you need a broiler, buy one. But if you don't need one, save the money. If necessary, make the salespeople explain to you why you need specific items of equipment they recommend for your menu items.

1. Consultants

In addition to salespeople, you might want to work with a restaurant consultant who can lay out your kitchen and dining areas for the greatest efficiency. By saving kitchen space, you can add to your seating area.

These consultants will also prepare a list of needed equipment and give advice about your seating area decor so it will suit your menu and type of service and customers. The few thousand dollars that you spend in consulting fees might well save you more than this in equipment budget reductions and increased sales volume over the long run.

2. Doing it yourself

You may want to do your own study of kitchen and dining room layout and design, with its related equipment and furnishing requirements.

This is a fascinating and complex area. Many specialized books have been written on the topic; some may be available in your local library. If you are close to a college that offers courses in hotel/restaurant administration, they are sure to have these books in their library and perhaps available for sale in their student bookstore.

The following books are a good resource.

(a) *A Modern Guide to Foodservice Equipment* by A.C. Avery. (New York: Van Nostrand Reinhold, 1985).

(b) *Manual of Equipment and Design for the Foodservice Industry* by Carl Scriven and James Stevens. (New York: Van Nostrand Reinhold, 1989).

(c) *Tabletop Presentations — A Guide for the Foodservice Professional* by Irving J. Mills. (New York: Van Nostrand Reinhold, 1989).

9
MARKET ANALYSIS

Every restaurant must be concerned with its market. The word "market" is defined in terms of people, their money, and their desire to exchange it for your food and service.

A restaurant's market is generally limited to a particular area (e.g., a community or a town), and it may be further limited by such things as competition and customers' preferences. Market analysis is based on the assumption that your restaurant must be developed around the customers' wants and needs in order to satisfy those customers. Customers are, therefore, the reason for being in business.

It is the marketing process that will eventually determine whether or not your restaurant is successful. It involves finding out what the customer wants, designing your restaurant and its menu to meet these wants, analyzing existing restaurants with reference to current consumer desires, determining the profit you want, establishing prices to achieve this profit, and creating and implementing an advertising/sales effort that will make potential customers aware of your restaurant.

The ultimate objective is the satisfaction of the consumer at a profit to you. Too many restaurateurs put the cart before the horse. They open a restaurant and then look for a market that they can sell to. Their emphasis is incorrectly on the need to sell rather than on the customers' desires.

a. MARKET ANALYSIS

Before you open a new restaurant, have a survey done. This survey will ultimately serve to determine if your sales goal can be met, and it will aid in your financial planning (see chapter 10). For a large restaurant, you may need to use specialists in market research to provide you with pertinent market information and to develop a specific market forecast and action plan to serve that market.

1. Develop a questionnaire

If you are going to be dealing primarily with the local pedestrian traffic, you might be able to design a simple questionnaire that you can administer yourself. It will provide you with information about your potential customers' needs. A typical, simple questionnaire for a take-out restaurant is illustrated in Sample #2.

Since it would be physically impossible, and unnecessary, to survey the entire local population with your questionnaire, only a small segment of that market need be sampled. A good representative sample, in most cases, would be from 100 to 300 potential customers. You could reach the sample by mailing out questionnaires or by interviewing on the telephone or on the street.

The results of the questionnaires, once tabulated, should provide you with sufficient highlights to indicate the direction your restaurant should be going in and your potential market size.

2. Traffic counts

In some situations, traffic counts (pedestrian and/or vehicular) can provide information on likely market size. You might be able to obtain vehicular traffic counts from your local city hall engineering department.

SAMPLE #2
MARKET ANALYSIS QUESTIONNAIRE

QUESTIONNAIRE

If you use a take-out restaurant in this area, which one is it?_____

Why do you use that one? _____

Do you walk or drive there? _____

At what time of the day do you usually go there? _____

How often have you been there in the past month? _____ year? _____

How do you rate that restaurant on the following:

	Good	Average	Poor
Food quality	_____	_____	_____
Price	_____	_____	_____
Cleanliness	_____	_____	_____
Service	_____	_____	_____

In a new take-out restaurant in this area, what type of food would you like to see?
_____

In a new take-out restaurant in this area, what features would you like to see?
_____
_____

Any other comments?
_____
_____
_____
_____
_____
_____
_____
_____

Alternatively, you can make the count yourself; take counts at different times of day and different days of the week to obtain realistic averages.

Not all passers-by will be potential customers. For example, pedestrians on their way to and from work may not be potential customers for your restaurant.

b. MARKET RESEARCH

In other cases, in-depth market research may be necessary to support your sales projections, to demonstrate that there is a large enough market to provide you with sufficient customers, and to show potential lenders that your sales projections are realistic.

1. Identify your trading area

In market research, you need to define your restaurant's trading area. The definition of your trading area will show you how many people live and/or work within it. That does not mean these people will all be customers of your restaurant. Only a certain proportion of them are potential restaurant customers, and because of competition from other restaurants in your trading area you can only expect to obtain a share of that market.

For most restaurants whose customers arrive by automobile, the trading area is within a 3- to 5-mile radius of your restaurant's location. In rural areas, the trading area might be as much as 60 minutes' driving distance. If your customers are mostly pedestrians, the trading area will be within 10 minutes' walking time of your location.

Your trading area should normally provide at least 50% of the restaurant's total business. However, there are exceptions to this rule of thumb. Some restaurants have two trading areas. For example, a shopping center restaurant might have visitors to the center as their luncheon trade and residents of the area (who are not visiting the center for shopping purposes) as their dinner trade. Also, some restaurants do not have a trading area that is within a limited distance of the operation. For example, a restaurant on a major highway may have little trade from its surrounding area and have as its market auto travelers who are simply passing through the area to a distant destination.

2. Use a map

A good way to analyze your potential trading area is to obtain a map of it and color in where you think the boundaries are. On the map you can also color in major highways that generate traffic that could provide you with customers. You can also indicate on it surrounding businesses whose employees could be potential customers.

Depending on the circumstances you can also show on the map any attractions (museums, sports centers, historic sites) whose visitors again might be potential customers. On this map you should also show locations of direct competitors (those that most closely duplicate your proposed type of operation) since knowledge about those competitors is also part of market research.

For example, if a trading area with a population of 10,000 can only support two restaurants of your kind, and there are already two in business, you would have to seriously consider whether a third could survive. Alternatively, if the two already there are surviving only marginally because of poor management or other reasons, you could possibly move in and take away sufficient business to thrive.

Finally, on this map you might want to indicate barriers that might restrict potential customers' movements. These barriers might be natural ones such as rivers or lakes, or constructed ones such as businesses or institutions that take up a large amount of space, one-way or dead-end streets, or busy highways that pedestrians and/or auto travelers avoid having to cross.

3. Research the demographics

In addition to knowing the boundaries of your normal trading area, you also need to know as much as possible about the demographics of the people living and/or working there. Demographics are statistical information about people such as their age, sex, marital status, average family size, average household income, education levels, ethnic origin, and average annual spending on dining out.

Demographics are important because they will indicate if there are sufficient people of the right type to support your proposed restaurant and if they are likely to have the desire to do so. If there are not enough people in the primary trading area to support your proposed restaurant or if they do not have enough spending power, then you would have to go beyond your primary trading area to attract customers — and this may be very difficult to do.

If your restaurant is going to cater to the business trade, then your demographic research must investigate such things as business hours, number of employees working in the area, and the dining pattern of those employees. For example, do they bring their own meals with them, eat at company cafeterias, or patronize local restaurants?

Similar types of analysis need to be done for public institutions (schools, hospitals, government offices) in your trading area, as well as for entertainment, cultural, and recreational centers.

Housing patterns can also be important in demographic research. Housing can be categorized as single-family homes, adult-only apartments, family apartments, adult-only condominiums, family condominiums, boarding or rooming houses, and so forth.

People who use one type of housing often have different dining out habits than those who use another type of housing.

4. Identify common characteristics

Knowing the demographics of the people in your trading area allows you to sort them into smaller groups according to certain characteristics (demographics) they have in common.

For example, you might find that most of the people living in your trading area are couples who have children who have grown up and left home, have above average incomes, and dine out on average three times a week. Obviously, this provides you with a larger market to draw from than if those people were couples who had on average two children per family, were below average in income, and seldom dined out.

Similarly, if you are planning an ethnic restaurant you will want to locate in an area where people of that ethnic origin live. Their common traditions and shared taste in food should provide you with plenty of potential customers.

Demographic data can be helpful in determining such matters as the type of restaurant you wish to operate (if you have not already made that decision), the type of menu you will offer, and menu item prices. It will also be useful in preparing a marketing plan so you can attract sufficient customers to make your operation successful.

5. Sources of demographic data

You can obtain demographic data about a trading area in many ways. For example, the federal government conducts a national census every few years. Census information provides demographic information that is publicly available in libraries. Other sources of information are:

(a) City and/or regional planning or economic development departments

(b) Local Chambers of Commerce

(c) Government publications

(d) Local restaurant associations

(e) Local university research studies

(f) Public agencies and organizations such as school boards and hospitals that analyze age and income demographics for their own forecasting and budgeting purposes

(g) Post office marketing departments that do their own demographic studies to help them analyze the information for direct mail purposes

(h) Real estate firms generally will have good information on housing, family sizes, income levels, and similar information

(i) Market research firms and/or advertising agencies may have information readily available for your trading area, and if not they can obtain it for you, usually at a cost

(j) Local radio and/or television stations and local newspapers do a great deal of local demographic research because this tells them who their listeners, viewers, or readers are

From a history of the demographics in your trading area you can also determine trends. For example, census data might show that the ethnic origin of people living in your trading area has been slowly changing. You can then project the trend of this change into the future to help you make decisions and plan for the future.

6. Verify demographic data

You can verify some of your demographic research findings and at the same time make yourself more familiar with your trading area by doing the following:

(a) Drive round your primary trading area to view such things as the homes (are they well maintained?), the quality of the environment, and similar matters.

(b) Visit local supermarkets and retail shops. Are the local area shoppers typical (in such matters as ages and family sizes) of what your research tells you?

(c) Determine by observation the average supermarket "bag value" (amount of money spent). If this is high, this can support demographic data that shows above average incomes. If the spending is low, this can indicate that average income is low and may mean that shoppers are living from paycheck to paycheck and that trading area inhabitants may not be good potential restaurant customers.

7. Customer profiles

A study of the demographics in your local trading area will also allow you to develop a potential customer profile including the type of person (for example, average age and income) that is to be typical of your customers. This customer profile can also be useful to you after you are in business since you can then compare your actual customers with this profile to see how well they fit and, over time, determine how that profile may be changing.

8. Find a gap

If you find that you are going to be competing in a market that is successfully filled by other restaurants, you may have a problem. It is best if you can find a gap that is not being filled by others. Ask yourself what unique menu items or services you can offer that differ from what others are offering.

9. Analyze your market

Your general market survey should provide you with answers to the following typical questions:

(a) What is the market size?

(b) Is it growing?

(c) What is the market's geographical distribution?

(d) What share of the market can you obtain?

(e) What type of restaurant is it interested in?

(f) Why is it interested in this type of restaurant?

(g) What price is it prepared to pay?

(h) How frequently will it patronize your restaurant?

(i) How will you provide the market with information about your food and services?

c. MARKET SEGMENT

These questions are very broad in nature and need to be refined to produce more specific information that allows market segmentation. In other words, it is unlikely an individual restaurant will sell to a broad range of possible users or customers.

The product that you sell has a major impact in determining who your customers will be. For example, a gourmet restaurant will be patronized by a narrower segment of the market than a coffee shop.

1. Quality

Quality of food plays an important role. A standard commercial or family restaurant will cater to a different segment of the population than a restaurant appealing to a specific ethnic group or a health-conscious clientele.

2. Price

Price is also a factor in market segmentation and can, to a degree, dictate the market segment you are dealing with. But price alone may not be the only significant factor. A special segment of the market will pay a higher price for similar menu items if the service in the restaurant is better. On the other hand, another segment of the market looks first for low prices and is less concerned about quality.

3. Competition

The existing competition may also dictate the market segment that you must concen-trate on. For example, if your choice of location for a Mexican food restaurant is an area already well served by firmly established Mexican food restaurants, you may have to change your thinking.

d. POTENTIAL SALES VOLUME

The main purpose of this market analysis is to establish your potential sales volume. This will become the forecast for your initial income statements.

One way to do this is to convert a percent of your traffic count or trading area population into potential sales. For example, if 2,600 pedestrians a day pass by your planned downtown location you might estimate that 5% of them could be customers for your restaurant and 5% x 2,600 = 130.

Assuming 80 of these would be lunch customers with an average spending (average check) of $5 for food, and 50 would be dinner customers with an average food check of $12, your daily sales would be:

$$80 \times \$5 = \$\ 400$$
$$50 \times \$12 = \underline{\ \ \ 600}$$
$$\text{TOTAL} \quad \underline{\$1,000}$$

If you were open 6 days a week or, let us say, 300 days a year, total annual sales could be forecast at $300,000. You can use this information to aid in preparing your financial plan, to be discussed in the next chapter.

e. SUMMARY

Some market research carried out in advance will at least show you that your business expectations were right. And if your restaurant is not going to be successful as originally conceived, it is better to find this out before, rather than after, the fact.

For example, if market research shows that your market is not nearly as large as you imagined, you might be able to scale down your plans until your market can be built up over time.

Well-documented market research can also be invaluable in obtaining financing to help you open your restaurant. Without market analysis documentation, a potential lender is going to view your plans a lot less favorably.

10
FINANCIAL PLAN

In order to start and survive in the restaurant business, you need a financial plan. You use a financial plan just like a map when traveling by car; it helps you get where you want to go. A properly prepared plan will guide you in operating your restaurant and help you allocate your resources effectively and profitably. A sound financial plan will allow you to raise the necessary funds to operate your restaurant successfully.

A combined market and financial plan (often referred to as a feasibility study by professionals who prepare them) is an in-depth analysis of the operational and financial feasibility of a new restaurant, rather than an entrepreneur's guess that a new restaurant will be economically viable.

A feasibility study, or plan, is not designed to prove that a new venture will be profitable. An independent plan professionally prepared by an impartial third party could result in either a positive or a negative recommendation. If you prepare your own plan, you should take the same hard approach. If the forecast results are negative, both you and any potential lenders of funds for your new restaurant should be happy the idea goes no further.

However, even if the forecast is positive, it is not a guarantee of success. A plan can only consider what is known at present and what may happen in the future. Since the future is impossible to forecast with absolute accuracy, and since so many unforeseen factors can come into play, there can be no guarantees.

In other words, a plan may reduce the risk of a particular new venture, but it does not eliminate that risk. Your completed market research results (discussed in the previous chapter) will form the foundation for your financial plan.

a. FINANCIAL STATEMENTS

You may choose to put together your own financial plan or you may have your accountant do it. Even in the latter case, it will help you if you know something about financial statements.

The two major parts of a financial statement are the balance sheet and the income statement. The balance sheet gives a picture of the financial position of a restaurant at a particular point in time. The income statement shows the operating results of the restaurant over a period of time.

The period of time referred to for the income statement usually ends on the date of the balance sheet:

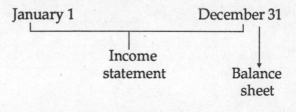

b. THE BALANCE SHEET

The debit portion of the balance sheet lists the assets or resources that a restaurant has. The credit portion lists liabilities (or debts of the company) and the shareholders' equity. On a balance sheet, total assets always equal total liabilities plus equity.

The asset portion of the balance sheet is generally broken down into three sections:

(a) Current assets

(b) Fixed or long-term assets

(c) Other assets

1. Current assets

Current assets are cash or items that can or will be converted into cash within a short period of time (usually a year or less). They include items such as cash on hand, cash in the bank, accounts receivable, inventories, and prepaid expenses (insurance, property tax, and similar items that have been paid in advance but not "used up" at the balance sheet date).

2. Fixed (long-term) assets

Fixed, or long-term assets, are those of a relatively permanent nature, not intended for sale, that are used in generating revenue. They include the land, building, fixtures, and equipment that are owned by the restaurant. These items are shown on the balance sheet at their cost.

From the cost figures for building and equipment (but not land) is deducted the accumulated depreciation. Accumulated depreciation reflects the estimated decline in value of the assets due to wear and tear, the passage of time, changed economic conditions, or other factors.

The difference between the asset cost figure and the accumulated depreciation is referred to as net book value. Net book value does not necessarily accurately reflect the current market or replacement value of the assets in question.

3. Other assets

If your restaurant has any other assets that do not fit into either the current or fixed categories, they are included here. An example might be leasehold costs or improvements.

If improvements are made to a building that you are leasing, these improvements are of benefit during the life of the restaurant or the remaining life of the lease. The costs should be spread over this life. This spreading of costs is much like depreciation, except that in cases such as leasehold property it is generally called amortization.

4. Total assets

The total of all the asset figures (current, fixed, and other) gives the total asset value, or total resources, of the restaurant.

5. Liabilities and owners' equity

The liabilities and owners' equity portion of the balance sheet shows how the assets have been financed or paid for. The liability section comprises two categories: current liabilities and long-term liabilities.

6. Current liabilities

Current liabilities are those debts that must be paid, or are expected to be paid, in less than a year. They include such items as accounts payable (for example for purchases of inventory or supplies), accrued expenses (wages/salaries due to employees, payroll tax deductions, and similar items), income tax payable, and the portion of any long-term loans or mortgages that are due within the next year.

7. Long-term liabilities

Long-term liabilities are the debts of the restaurant that are payable more than one year after the balance sheet date. Included in this category are mortgages and any similar long-term loans.

8. Owners' equity

In general terms, the owners' equity section of the balance sheet is the difference between the total assets and the total liabilities. It represents the equity, or the net worth, of the owners of the restaurant. In an incorporated company, the owners' equity is made up of two main items: capital (shares) and retained earnings.

Shares generally have a par, or stated, value. This par value multiplied by the number of shares actually issued gives the total value of capital on the balance sheet.

The other part of the owners' equity section of the balance sheet is retained earnings. Retained earnings are the link between the income statement and the balance sheet. For that reason, the retained earnings part of the owners' equity section of the balance sheet is discussed below, after you have had a chance to read about the income statement. A typical balance sheet is illustrated in Sample #3.

c. THE INCOME STATEMENT

The income statement shows the operating results of the restaurant for a period of time (month, quarter, half-year, or year).

Formal income statements are prepared at least once a year (this is required for income tax filing reasons, if for no other) and informal ones more frequently. The income statement shows income from sales (revenue) less any expenses made to achieve that revenue. An income statement for a restaurant is illustrated in Sample #4.

The amount of detail concerning revenue and expenses to be shown on the income statement depends on the type and size of the restaurant and on the needs of the owner/operator for either more or less information.

d. RETAINED EARNINGS

Usually the balance sheet and the income statement are accompanied by a statement of retained earnings. The statement of retained earnings is the place where the net profit of the restaurant (from the income statement) for a period of time (let us say a year) is added to the preceding year's figure of retained earnings to give the new total. In other words, the retained earnings are the accumulated net profits, less any losses, of the restaurant since it began.

The retained earnings are not necessarily represented by cash in the bank because the money may have been used for other necessities such as purchasing new equipment or refurbishing the restaurant.

A completed statement of retained earnings is illustrated in Sample #5. Note how the $66,000 of net profit from the income statement (Sample #4) has been transferred to the statement of retained earnings (Sample #5) and the year-end retained earnings figure of $229,000, transferred to the balance sheet (Sample #3).

e. FORECAST INCOME STATEMENT

Prior to opening you need to forecast your first year's income statement. In forecasting sales for your restaurant, use the following formula to calculate sales for a month:

Restaurant seats x Seat turnover x
Average check x Days in month

Apply this formula separately to each meal period because seat turnover (the number of times on average that each seat is occupied) varies by meal period as does the average check. (The average check is what each customer, on average, is expected to spend.) Also, you may be open for some meals seven days a week and for other meals only five or six.

For example, if you plan a 100-seat restaurant, intend to be open for breakfast seven days a week, expect breakfast seat turnover of 2 and average breakfast check of $4.25, total breakfast sales for the month of June would be —

100 x 2.0 x $4.25 x 30 = $25,500

Similar calculations can be made for the lunch and dinner periods, and even for coffee break periods if these are likely to add significantly to overall sales. In this way you can arrive at total sales forecast for the month of June. Calculate sales for the other months in a similar way so that you can arrive at total annual sales.

SAMPLE #3
BALANCE SHEET

RISSOLE RESTAURANT — Balance Sheet as at June 30, 199-

ASSETS

Current Assets

Cash		$ 8,000
Accounts receivable		3,000
Inventories		6,000
Prepaid expenses		5,000
Total current assets		$ 22,000

Fixed Assets

Land, at cost		$ 72,000
Building, at cost	$333,000	
Less: Accumulated depreciation	57,000	276,000
Equipment, at cost	$ 74,000	
Less: Accumulated depreciation	45,000	29,000
Total fixed assets		$377,000

Other Assets

Deferred expense		6,000
Total Assets		$405,000

LIABILITIES & OWNERS' EQUITY

Current Liabilities

Accounts payable		$ 9,000
Accrued expenses		4,000
Income tax payable		3,000
Current portion of mortgage		17,000
Total current liabilities		$ 33,000

Long-Term Liabilities

Mortgage on building	$140,000	
Less: current portion	17,000	123,000
Total Liabilities		$156,000

Owners' Equity

Capital - authorized 5,000 common shares @100 par value; issued and outstanding 200 shares	$ 20,000	
Retained earnings	229,000	249,000
Total Liabilities & Equity		$405,000

SAMPLE #4
INCOME STATEMENT

RISSOLE RESTAURANT	
Income Statement for Year Ending June 30, 199-	
Sales	$1,250,000
Cost of goods sold	450,000
Gross profit	$ 800,000
Operating expenses: (listed in detail)	668,000
Profit before income tax	$ 132,000
Income tax	66,000
Net profit	$ 66,000

SAMPLE #5
STATEMENT OF RETAINED EARNINGS

RISSOLE RESTAURANT	
Statement of Retained Earnings for Year Ending June 30, 199-	
Retained earnings beginning of year	$193,000
Add profit for year	66,000
	$259,000
Deduct dividends paid	30,000
Retained earnings June 30, 199-	$229,000

It is important to detail your sales calculations as carefully as possible because potential lenders (investors) will need to know how you arrived at total sales month by month and need to be assured you have not just pulled the numbers out of a hat.

The next step in mapping out a financial plan for your new restaurant is to obtain operating statistics for similar types of restaurants so that you can complete your first year's income statement. The kind of operating statistics you are looking for are the ratio of cost of sales (food cost) and other operating expenses to sales.

Try to get these statistics from similar restaurants now operating. If you are unable to get this information from restaurants with whom you are going to compete, try the following sources:

(a) Local Chamber of Commerce or Board of Trade

(b) Government departments of small business

(c) Financial institutions such as banks

(d) Restaurant management magazines

(e) The local restaurant association

(f) Local university and college departments teaching hotel/restaurant administration

For example, you can apply the food cost percent figure to the calculated potential sales to arrive at gross profit or margin. (See chapter 16 for a discussion of food costs.) From this you can deduct other operating expenses, including a reasonable salary for yourself, applying appropriate expense percent to sales figures for each separate expense to arrive at a net income or profit figure.

The net income should be sufficient to give you at least 10% return on your investment, otherwise you might be better to leave your investment funds in the bank and eliminate the risk of trying to run your own restaurant.

f. INVESTMENT REQUIRED

To see if the net profit is going to provide the suggested minimum 10% return, you must also determine what kind of total investment is required in the restaurant. Your investment costs might include the purchase of land at the location you want. This will be a known and fairly specific cost.

You may also need to purchase the building in which you are going to operate. Again, this will be a fairly specific and exact cost. In other cases, you may be constructing a building, in which case construction costs can be estimated using the approach suggested in chapter 7 and in Worksheet #2.

However, for most restaurants in leased premises, the major investment will be in equipment, furniture, and decor. Some cost guidelines for this investment were identified in chapter 8.

Nevertheless, even in rented premises, you will still have startup costs for improvements to the premises such as painting and decorating, building walls or partitions, and making plumbing or electrical changes. You will also probably need fixtures (such as lighting, counters, shelving, and indoor and outdoor signs).

All of these costs should be estimated. Use Worksheet #3 to summarize these costs.

In addition, you will also have to estimate your pre-opening costs. These are the costs that you incur prior to opening your door and making sales to provide a cash flow. These costs include such items as food and beverage inventories, payment for employees needed prior to opening, pre-opening advertising costs, and working capital you must have on hand.

You also need to forecast the operating costs for the first two or three months to make sure you have enough opening cash to pay these expenses until cash starts flowing into the restaurant.

Use Worksheet #4 to summarize your pre-opening and operating costs. Note that on this worksheet you should add 10% to the total of these costs for contingency purposes. It is easy to overestimate sales and underestimate costs; the contingency may help compensate for this.

g. FINANCIAL ANALYSIS

In a formal feasibility study for a major restaurant, you might need much more detail than has been suggested so far. In fact, the financial analysis section of a feasibility study is usually broken down into the following subsections:

(a) Capital investment required and tentative financing plan

(b) Projected income statements for at least the first year and for as far ahead as five years

(c) Projected cash flow statement for at least the first year and for as far ahead as five years

(d) An evaluation of the financial projections and the economic viability of the new restaurant

Since the preparation of the financial analysis can be a fairly complex matter that requires the expertise of someone with an accounting background, it is recommended that you use a professional consultant or accountant. Also, lenders from whom you wish to borrow money are more likely to be convinced to part with that money if the feasibility study is professionally prepared.

Finally, if the financial projections made by an impartial third party appear to be negative, it is better that you know this now rather than two or three years down the road after your restaurant is bankrupt.

WORKSHEET #3
FIXTURES AND EQUIPMENT ESTIMATES

ITEM	ESTIMATED COST	ITEM	ESTIMATED COST
Counters	$_____	Outdoor signs	$_____
Stands	$_____	Decorating/remodeling	$_____
Shelving	$_____	China, glassware, silverware	$_____
Cabinets	$_____	Uniforms	$_____
Tables	$_____	Kitchen equipment (see separate list)	$_____
Chairs	$_____		
Lighting	$_____		
Cash register	$_____	TOTAL — Enter on worksheet for pre-opening and operating expenses (see Worksheet #4)	$_____
Safe	$_____		
Office equipment	$_____		

WORKSHEET #4
PRE-OPENING AND OPERATING EXPENSES ESTIMATES

Estimated Monthly Operating Costs		Pre-opening Costs	
Owner/manager salary	$_____	Starting inventory	$_____
Other employee salary/wages	$_____	Advertising	$_____
Advertising	$_____	Legal and accounting	$_____
Delivery	$_____	License	$_____
Insurance	$_____	Utility deposit	$_____
Interest	$_____	Cash on hand	$_____
Legal and accounting	$_____	Other	$_____
License	$_____	Total of Operating and Pre-opening Costs	$_____
Maintenance	$_____	Add 10% for contingency	$_____
Supplies	$_____		
Telephone	$_____	**Fixtures and equipment total** (from Worksheet #3)	$_____
Utilities	$_____		
Other	$_____		
Total of above	$_____	**Total estimated investment required**	$_____
Multiply this total by 3	$_____		

11
EQUITY VERSUS DEBT FINANCING

Now that you know from your financial plan what total initial investment is required, and that you should be able to obtain a reasonable return on this investment, you can begin deciding how this investment will be financed. In general, there are two main sources of funding for any restaurant: debt and equity.

Equity financing is the money the owners of the business put up themselves. This may be in the form of shares (stock) that the business issues and that the owners invest in, or it could be in the form of loans to the business.

With debt financing, the lender does not have any equity or ownership in the restaurant and thus normally no active say in the day-to-day operations of the restaurant. Banks are one type of debt lender. Their return on their investment (loan) is the interest the business pays on the use of that money.

However, before you can raise any debt financing you will normally have to show potential lenders that you are willing to invest (and risk) money in the restaurant yourself. If you are not willing to invest in the restaurant yourself through your share (equity) ownership, then why should an outside lender invest in it?

a. EQUITY FINANCING

The equity investment could range from 10% to 50% of the total investment. The closer to 50% it is, the easier it will be to obtain debt financing and the higher your profits might be (since you will have less interest expense that will eat into those profits).

1. Personal funds

The most common source of equity capital is personal funds from savings. Over the past few years many entrepreneurs have been able to provide this initial equity because inflation caused an increase in the value of their homes, which could be remortgaged to provide instant cash.

2. Friends or relatives

This equity could be further increased from the savings of friends willing to invest in shares or loans, or even from relatives (love money). However, many otherwise successful small restaurants have had problems because friends or relatives were equity investors.

Mixing social or family relationships with business is always risky, particularly if the restaurant is not doing as well as everyone initially imagined, or if the terms and conditions of such loans are not clearly spelled out to prevent these lenders from becoming involved in day-to-day operations. Also, if a relative dies, the heirs may immediately demand their money back, with interest, under the threat of a lawsuit.

To avoid these problems, make sure any friend or family loans are covered by written agreements, preferably drawn up by a lawyer. In this way, agreements will at least be viewed by the lenders on a businesslike basis.

Agreement should be reached on such matters as rate of interest to be paid, when the loans will be retired (paid back), and any option you have to pay back early. Also covered should be the procedures that all parties will follow if loans become delinquent.

3. Shares

Unless your company is a proprietorship or partnership, it will have to issue some shares. In a one-person company, those shares will be held by you as owner. A larger company may possibly have several owners or shareholders, some of whom could be friends or relatives who want to invest in your new restaurant by purchasing shares rather than by making direct loans.

4. Loans versus shares

The total "equity" investment (i.e., the money you can raise by not going to outside lenders such as banks) could be in the form of loans, or common stock or shares in the company, or a combination of loans and shares. How the owners' or equity investors' investment in the company is structured will vary in each situation.

Generally speaking, the advantage of taking the money in loans is that the business can pay back the loans without the lenders having to pay tax, other than personal tax on interest received from the company before all the loan is finally paid off.

If the money is in the form of shares, the lenders will find it much more difficult to withdraw their money since shares must be sold to someone else, or be repurchased by the company, and may be subject to personal capital gains tax by the shareholders.

On the other hand, equity investor loans (that is, loans to the business by its owners), because of the ease with which they can be repaid, are looked upon with skepticism by banks and other debt investors since it would be feasible for the business to borrow money from a bank and use the cash to pay back equity investor loans.

The long-term debt investors may therefore place restrictions or conditions on when and how your restaurant can pay off shareholder loans, redeem shares, or possibly even pay dividends on shares. These restrictions or conditions are imposed to protect long-term debt investors.

Seek the advice of a tax accountant before you decide on your financing plans since your personal tax situation, and that of any other equity investors, and the degree of financial success of the business, can have a bearing on whether the shareholders' investment should be in the form of loans or purchase of shares.

b. DEBT FINANCING

The other type of financing available to a restaurant is debt. An important aspect of debt is the interest rate you will have to pay on this borrowed money.

1. Interest

Banks and other financial institutions vary interest rates according to money market conditions. The rates can change frequently. The prime rate is generally the lowest rate available. Rates increase above that depending on the specific business, its credit rating, its size, and other factors.

Rates also vary depending on the customer. Because of the risk involved to the lender, small restaurants in need of bank credit probably pay rates that tend to be among the highest.

Lending rates for long-term loans (more than three years) are sometimes higher than current short-term rates since they are fixed for the term of the loan. Because of this, and the fact that lenders have been hurt in volatile money markets, it is now often difficult to obtain a fixed interest rate on a long-term loan.

2. Balloon payments

Long-term loans may also be subject to two-year or three-year terms and balloon payments. A balloon payment simply means that at the end of the term, the lender calls in the loan and you must negotiate, usually on the lender's terms, a new loan for the amount still owing on the old one.

3. Variable rate

Variable rate long-term loans are not uncommon. A variable rate loan simply means that the interest rates are adjustable by the lender, as frequently as monthly, either up or down depending on money market conditions. These market conditions can take into consideration the current inflation rate and the market's expectation of the future inflation rate.

4. Lender competition

Since banks are in competition with other banks or other financial lending institutions, these interest rates are competitive, just as your menu prices have to be. Therefore, in seeking a loan, you should search out the lender with the most favorable lending rate and conditions, just as you would expect astute customers to seek you out if you offered the best quality at a competitive price.

5. Security

Another important aspect of borrowing money by debt is security. Most lenders will require some sort of security for loans made to restaurants. For intermediate and long-term loans, this security will be quite specific (see chapter 12). For short-term loans of a year or less, this security will probably take the form of a personal guarantee.

6. Personal guarantees

Even if your restaurant is incorporated, the lender may require this guarantee or endorsement of the loan in case your company does not meet its debt obligations. This means that if your restaurant defaults on its repayments, the lender can claim against your personal assets such as your savings, your home, your car, or other personal belongings.

Normally, particularly if your case for a loan is not a strong one, you will have little choice but to provide this personal guarantee or endorsement. If there are other shareholders in the company, they might also be required to sign guarantees.

In some cases, where neither you nor other principals in the company can provide sufficient security to the lender you may be asked to find an outside guarantor. If your case is so weak that you need an outside guarantor, you might question whether or not you should really be taking the loan.

This guarantee may be limited or unlimited. A limited guarantee gives the lender the right to demand that you repay, on request, the amount owing on that specific loan. An unlimited guarantee gives the lender the right to demand that you repay, on request, all loans due to that lender. Obviously, it is preferable for you to have a limited guarantee.

7. Guarantee release

Make sure that when any guaranteed loan is paid off you obtain a release from the guarantee. If a personal guarantee is required by the lender in addition to other security, try to negotiate a guarantee only for the amount of the shortfall and not for the full amount of the loan.

Also, if you or any other equity investors made a direct loan to the company and were obliged by the debt lender to sign a postponement of claim for your own loan, make sure that the postponement of claim is also canceled.

Similarly, if during the period of the debt, restrictions were placed on payment of dividends to you, or if life insurance policies were assigned to the lender, have these restrictions removed and/or the policies changed.

8. Other alternatives

You may be able to obtain a loan, if by no other method, by assigning your savings account to the lender as security. While it is assigned, your withdrawals from it will be limited.

Another alternative is to raise cash from your life insurance policy. However, instead of raising cash from your insurance company based on your policy's paid up cash value, you may be able to raise the cash by assigning it to a bank since it may be easier and speedier to obtain the cash that way.

Finally, if you have marketable stocks and bonds, you may be able to use them as security or collateral for a loan. These would have to be gilt-edged stocks, and the maximum you could expect might be up to 75% of their market value. If you have government bonds, the percentage might go as high as 90. If the market value on your stocks and bonds drops while they are secured, you may at that time have to put up additional collateral or reduce the loan.

12
SHORT-, INTERMEDIATE-, AND LONG-TERM FINANCING

One basic rule of finance is that short-term requirements for cash should be provided by short-term financing, and longer-term requirements by intermediate- or long-term financing.

If this rule is not followed, you might end up with a financing imbalance. This could happen, for example, if you made a one-year bank loan and used this money to buy kitchen equipment.

If that happened, you might find yourself short of cash to purchase inventory, carry receivables, pay your payables, and even short of cash to pay back the one-year loan! You could even be forced into liquidation or bankruptcy in such a situation.

a. SHORT-TERM FINANCING

In most restaurants that are being started the greatest need is for short-term financing, generally considered to be funding required for a period of less than a year. In short-term financing the lender will tend to place greater emphasis on your balance sheet in order to see if, in case of your restaurant's liquidation, current assets would provide sufficient funds to repay the debt. Some of the various methods of short-term financing are as follows.

1. Trade credit

Surprisingly, the most common means of short-term financing is trade credit or financial assistance from suppliers with whom you do business. The reason for this is that most suppliers do not demand cash on delivery other than in those cases where a restaurant has a reputation for delinquency in payment of accounts.

Usually a bill or invoice for purchases is sent at the month end. A 30-day payment period for items purchased at the beginning of a month means that you use the supplies received without cost for anywhere up to 60 days.

This type of trade credit is an important source of cash for a restaurant. Even if you had the cash to pay the bill at the time it was received, it may not be wise to do so. As long as there is no penalty imposed, you are free to let your cash sit in the bank and collect interest until the invoice has to be paid. This is another source of profit to you.

This finance source, sometimes called "open credit," can be useful in financing the inventory of a new restaurant.

For example, if you purchased $2,500 of inventory, you might put up $1,000 cash and owe the suppliers the balance to be paid 30 days later. During that 30 days, most if not all of that inventory will be sold at a profit and you will have the cash to pay off the $1,500 owed. This cycle can be repeated ad infinitum.

Unfortunately, many new restaurants are on a cash on delivery (COD) basis. This means that you do not receive any trade credit. Cash must be paid at the time of delivery.

But, by paying cash on delivery for initial orders from suppliers to establish and maintain good supplier relations, you can build up a solid credit base with a supplier.

You should also be ready to provide a supplier with credit references in order to establish your trade credit. Most larger suppliers will have credit departments, or will employ an agency, to check on your credit status if you are a new customer desiring trade credit.

Also, as you build up your credit record with suppliers, you might later be able to negotiate more favorable trade credit terms, such as extending the time period before payment is required, or receiving a discount in invoices paid more promptly.

Sometimes a supplier may offer both a credit period and a cash discount. One common type is 2/10, net 30. This means that you are offered a 2% discount off the invoice price if the bill is paid within 10 days. If the bill is not paid within the 10-day period, it must be paid within a further 20 days but without discount. This type of arrangement is made to encourage you to pay bills promptly.

With a 2/10, net 30 arrangement, you must seriously consider the cost of not taking the discount. For example, if you make a $1,000 purchase and pay within 10 days, the amount to be paid is $980. If the discount is not taken you, in effect, have the use of this $980 for a further 20 days. However, the cost of this would be:

$$\frac{\$20}{\$980} \times \frac{365}{20} = 37.2\%$$

This is an expensive form of financing. Even if you are short of cash, it might be wise to borrow $980 from the bank to pay within the discount period, since the bank interest would probably be considerably less than 37%.

If the nature of your restaurant is seasonal, you might find it difficult to pay all bills in the off season when they are due. In such cases, it might be wise to prearrange for a longer payment period with suppliers whose financial resources allow them to extend longer credit, instead of risking the loss of your credit. Alternative-ly, arrangements could be made with a lending institution to borrow funds for the interim to pay bills within the normal payment period.

You should also recognize that trade credit is not absolutely "free." The supplier who extends credit also has financing costs, which must be paid out of revenue from the products sold. In other words, the cost is included in the selling prices. Where competition exists among suppliers, however, this hidden cost should be small.

2. Short-term or operating loans

Short-term or operating loans are for financing inventory and accounts receivable and other items requiring working capital during peak periods.

The main sources of short-term loans are commercial banks or similar financial institutions. Using a short-term loan is a good way to establish credit with a bank. A lender who is considering a short-term loan will be interested in your restaurant's liquidity. If you have a healthy working capital, your restaurant will be a good prospect for a short-term loan.

Short-term loans are usually negotiated for specific periods of time (for example 30, 60, or 90 days) and may be repayable in a lump sum at the end of the period, or in periodic installments such as monthly. If you have adequate collateral, short-term loans of up to a year can sometimes be negotiated.

Each separate borrowing is usually covered by a promissory note (a form of contract spelling out the interest rate and terms of the loan), and the interest rate is frequently subject to change, particularly in erratic money markets.

A personal guarantee by you and/or your spouse (when personal assets are registered in the spouse's name) may be required.

The interest rate on term loans is usually a stated annual interest rate. The stated rate may differ from the effective (or true) rate if the loan is discounted. Discounting means that the interest on the loan is deducted in advance.

If you take out a $1,000 bank loan at the beginning of the year, to be repaid at the end of the year at a discount (interest) rate of 15%, you would receive $850 ($1,000, less 15% of $1,000, or $150), and repay $1,000 at the end of the year. Since you have only $850, the effective interest rate is

$$\frac{\$150}{\$850} \times 100 = 17.6\%$$

Tables are available from which an exact rate of interest can be determined under various circumstances.

In all cases where money is being borrowed, and particularly where you are shopping around for the best rate, it is important to know what the effective interest rate is.

3. Line of credit

A line of credit is an agreement between you and a bank, or similar financial institution, specifying the maximum amount of credit (overdraft) the bank will allow you at any one time.

Credit lines are usually established for one-year periods, subject to annual renegotiation and renewal, with the bank taking your accounts receivable and inventory as security.

The amount of credit is based on the bank's assessment of the creditworthiness of your restaurant and its credit requirements. This type of loan is sometimes called a demand loan since the bank can demand that it be repaid immediately without notice. However, this would not happen under normal circumstances.

A restaurant with a line of credit of any sizeable amount is generally required to keep a deposit balance with the lender.

This deposit balance is usually proportionate to the amount of the line of credit.

For example, it might be stipulated by the lender at 10% to 15% of the line of credit amount. This percentage might vary with the money market.

Since the deposit amount is generally in an account that pays little or no interest it favors the bank and increases the effective interest rate you are paying on any money used from your line of credit. Some banks accept fees or a higher interest rate in lieu of a compensating balance.

The establishment of a line of credit protects you since normally the lender will not reduce or cancel the line of credit without good cause. However, the lender will keep an eye on your financial statements and economic and other factors that might influence your restaurant's operations and change the lender's view of the appropriateness of your particular line of credit.

A line of credit is useful for a restaurant with a peak seasonal financial need. In such a situation, a line of credit is the usual answer to cash needs.

4. Other loans

Some other types of short-term loans that your financial institution might offer are collateral loans, character loans, chattel mortgages, and floating charge debentures. Each one of these loans has its own unique characteristics and restrictions. Your bank manager or financial adviser will be able to recommend the best short-term financing plan for you and give you additional details.

b. INTERMEDIATE-TERM FINANCING

Somewhere between short- and long-term financing is a need at times for intermediate-term financing for items not generally purchased on a regular basis, such as equipment and fixtures for your new restaurant.

When considering an intermediate-term loan, lending companies rely on indications of your restaurant's profitability and ability to repay. These indications are provided by income statement and cash flow forecasts for the next several years as long as these forecasts are reasonable and not made on the basis of overestimated sales and underestimated expenses. Intermediate-term financing can be in the form of a term loan or installment financing.

1. Term loans

Term loans are usually obtained from banks or similar financial institutions, but, unlike short-term loans, are usually arranged to cover the purchase of basic inventory, leasehold improvements, and assets such as furniture, fixtures, and equipment. Generally 60% to 75% of the cost of these items can be obtained through term loans.

Term loans are usually repaid in regular installments of principal and interest over the life of the loan, which is usually less than the life of the assets for which financing is required. Term loans could vary in length from one to five years. The interest rate is usually a percentage point or more higher than that for a short-term loan made to the same borrower.

The periodic payments on term loans can be geared to the restaurant's cash flow ability to repay. In some cases, only the interest portion of such loans is payable in the first year or two. Payments could be monthly, quarterly, semi-annually, or annually. Payments are calculated so that the debt is repaid (amortized) by a specific date.

If the periodic payments do not completely amortize the debt by the maturity date, the final payment will be larger than the previous periodic payments. This larger, final payment is known as a "balloon" payment. Term loans sometimes allow early repayment without penalty.

Interest rates may also be negotiable. As long as you adhere to the terms of the loan, you can generally be assured that no payments other than the regular installment ones will be required before the due date of the loan.

Term loans have an advantage in that they develop a lender/borrower relationship over a number of years that can be useful in future financial matters, including advice from the lender concerning preferable future financing arrangements that you could make.

Most term loans are only offered to companies with profit histories whose current or projected financial statements demonstrate an ability to repay. For that reason a term loan may not be easy to find for a new restaurant.

2. Installment financing

As an alternative to a term loan, installment financing could be used to finance the purchase of equipment of various kinds, dining room furnishings, and fixtures (such as counters and shelves) where term loans are unavailable.

By using an equipment loan you can retain precious working capital. Lenders will generally finance from 60% to 80% of the asset's value. The balance is your down payment. Although some furniture and equipment sales companies may finance this way directly, others will sell to a financing company that, in turn, will do the installment financing.

Many supply companies will act as an intermediary between you and the finance company to coordinate the arrangement. In other cases you may have to shop around to arrange your own installment financing.

Since the assets being financed generally have a life of 5 to 10 years, and since the financing agency runs a relatively high risk because of the very low value of secondhand fixtures and equipment (and thus its low value as collateral), the length of life of such financing is usually from 3 to 7 years with repayments of principal and interest made monthly. The interest rate is generally much higher than with term loans; it could run as much as 5 or 6 points over prime.

Installment loans are generally secured by a chattel mortgage (a lien on the assets financed), which can be registered and which permits the seller or lending company to sell the liened assets if the installment payments are in default.

Alternatively, the lender's security could be a conditional sales contract, whereby the seller or lender retains title to the assets until you have satisfied all the terms of the contract.

The installment loan agreement usually binds you to maintaining working capital at an agreed level and to obtaining lender approval before making any capital expenditure over a specified limit. It might also limit the amount that can be paid in salaries and bonuses, and require that assets be kept free of encumbrances.

Finally, the agreement might require that a portion of profits be applied to loan repayments above and beyond the amount stipulated in your note payable securing the installment loan.

c. LONG-TERM FINANCING

Where a long-term loan is required (for example, to purchase land or to build or purchase a building), it will probably be in the form of a mortgage. If you do not plan to own land and/or a building for your restaurant, you can skip the rest of this chapter.

A mortgage is a grant, by the borrower to a creditor or lender, of preference or priority in a particular asset. This asset is usually some type of real estate. If the borrower is in default (for example, for non-payment of interest and/or principal owing), the creditor holding the mortgage is entitled to force the sale of the asset or assets pledged as security. Proceeds of the sale go to the holder of the first mortgage before any other creditors receive anything.

If another creditor has a mortgage on the same asset or assets, he or she is classified as a second mortgage holder, and ranks below the first mortgage holder but above a third mortgage holder (if one exists) or other creditors of the borrower in default. The legal procedure by which the first mortgage holder can force the sale is called foreclosure.

1. Requirements

Before lending money, a mortgage lender considers factors such as your track record. If you have a proven record of five years or more of successful experience in business, you are more likely to obtain funds at a reasonable rate than is a novice.

Lenders are also concerned about the amount of equity invested by the owner. This equity usually takes the form of a direct cash investment in shares if the company is incorporated. If you do not make this equity investment, the mortgage lender is taking a high risk. Generally, such equity needs to be a minimum of 25% to 30% of the required financing. In other words, if the total investment cost is $500,000 you need $125,000 to $150,000 of personal cash investment.

A prospective lender is also concerned that proper accounting procedures, particularly for cost control, are used. Lenders frequently require audited financial statements at least yearly but sometimes more frequently. This allows them to read possible danger signs before it is too late.

Some lenders carry out on-site inspections of properties in which they have investments to ensure that the property is not run down and that it is being maintained adequately. This ensures that their investment is protected. In some cases, the mortgage investor may stipulate a percentage of annual revenue that must be spent on property maintenance.

2. Loan terms

Generally, first mortgages can be obtained for up to 70% or 75% of the appraised value of the land and/or building offered as security for the loan. If the land is leased, the mortgage is usually obtainable only on the appraised value of the building. The term is usually for a maximum of 20 to 25 years. However, it can be as short as 10 years.

Repayment of loans is generally made in equal monthly payments of principal and interest. These payments are calculated so that, at the stated interest rate, the regular payments will completely amortize (pay off) the mortgage by the end of its life.

3. Early payment

Most first mortgage loans do not permit any early payment for at least the first several years. Thus you are locked in for that period and cannot benefit if interest rates decline.

Where prepayment is permitted, the mortgagor may impose a penalty. The penalty is usually a percentage of the balance still owing, and the percentage may decline as time goes by. You might be prepared to pay such a penalty. For example, if the initial mortgage has an 18% interest rate, and current rates are 14%, you might be able to negotiate a new loan with a new lender, and use part of the proceeds to pay off the remaining balance of the initial mortgage plus penalty. The penalty imposition may be more than offset by the interest reduction over the term of the new mortgage.

4. Call provision

A call provision allows the lender, after a stated number of years, to ask for complete repayment of the mortgage. The lender and borrower then renegotiate a new mortgage at a new interest rate for a further stipulated period of time. A lender would probably call a loan if interest rates had increased since the original mortgage agreement was signed.

5. Other compensation

Some lenders also require additional compensation such as a fee, discount, or bonus. For example, a $10,000 bonus on a $250,000 mortgage means you receive only $240,000 but must pay back principal and interest on the $250,000. Such front-end "loads" obviously raise the effective interest rate.

Other lenders may ask for an equity participation. This equity participation increases the lender's return on the investment and, at the same time, dilutes your return on investment. Equity might take the form of a percentage of annual revenue, or an investment in common shares.

6. Joint venture

In some cases, the lender might enter into a joint venture agreement with you. Such an agreement might provide you with some equity funds (while giving up part of equity control) as well as mortgage funds.

In other cases, the mortgage investor might supply 100% of the total project cost for which he or she receives a substantial equity position. This might significantly reduce your capital outlay, and at the same time reduce your risk, control, and potential future income.

7. Equipment and fixtures

Most long-term mortgage lenders will not normally finance any portion of your equipment and fixtures. The prime reason is that mortgage lenders are in the long-term loan business, and furniture and equipment have a relatively short life.

However, despite this, they will sometimes attempt to obtain a first mortgage on these chattels (in addition to the long-term mortgage on the assets that they have financed).

In this way, if the first mortgage lender has to foreclose, he or she is sure that the equipment and fixtures will not be removed and that the restaurant can continue to operate.

8. Second mortgages

Second mortgages are also used for financing land and building. A second mortgage lender takes a second lien on the property mortgaged. The loan amount is generally limited to 5% to 15% of the appraised value of the property, and loan terms usually range from 5 to 15 years.

Second mortgage interest rates are generally three to four points above first mortgage rates because of the additional risk involved. Repayments are made over the life of the loan in equal monthly installments of principal and interest.

An excessive second mortgage can be risky to both you and the lender because of potential cash flow problems if the restaurant is not successful.

13

BORROWING MONEY

Knowing what's involved in securing financing can give you a distinct advantage. The most important fact to remember is that you are in competition with other people and other businesses for the same money. Being prepared, understanding the procedures involved, and being familiar with the different types of financing available are the first steps in demonstrating good management of a financial proposal.

You should also understand that banks and other financial institutions are no different than you; they are in competition with each other in the same way you are with your competitors.

Banks make money by lending money at a profit. If they don't lend money, they don't make that profit. If you don't sell your menu items, you won't make a profit. However, the bank has to assess the risk before lending its money.

Risk is the degree of danger the lender has of losing funds loaned to you. Interest is what you pay a lender for the use of borrowed funds. Normally, the higher the risk, the higher the interest rate. Decisions made by bankers are based on their judgment of the viability of your proposal. This judgment follows no secret formula (since banks do make errors in lending money that they cannot collect). However, bankers do use certain basic information to determine risk and make their decisions.

a. PREPARING THE PAPERWORK

The style and content of a loan application are of major importance when asking for a loan. To make the best impression on those approached for funding, it is critical to have all the facts properly documented. Regardless of the type of loan, the information required by the lender is basically the same.

The lender wants to know who you are, what your plans are, and what these plans will do for the business. The preparation of this information, in answer to the lender's questions, and the analysis that backs it up, is quite simple.

In particular, a potential lender is likely to be interested in why you decided on this particular type of restaurant and in that specific location. Is it because you have experience with that type of food or in working in that type of restaurant? Do you perceive a need for that type of restaurant in the location selected? Or do you have some other reason? Wherever possible, support your reason with facts and figures.

Further, a potential lender will be interested in who the landlord is (if you are renting your premises) and what the rental terms are. If the lease has been signed, attach a copy of it.

Explain what your deadline is for starting your new operation because that shows how quickly any financing has to be arranged.

Also, explain why you think your restaurant will succeed when most new restaurants do not. Reasons could be location, high potential sales, an unusual menu that market research shows will be accepted, a rapidly growing trading area that can easily support a new restaurant, and so forth. If you do not have good factually based reasons to support why you think you will be successful, you (and potential lenders) should question whether you are making the right move.

1.   Resume of the owners

The lender wants to know something about you (and any other owners), such as your education and experience (or lack of it) and how this will be valuable to the business. The lender wants to be assured of your managerial skills, particularly if they are in the restaurant business. Alternatively, a past track record demonstrating ability in matters such as production, marketing, financing, and similar areas and a demonstrated understanding of how these are related to the restaurant you propose starting are some determining factors in assessing your management ability.

The lender needs this information to size up your character and to assess your honesty, reliability, trustworthiness, responsibility, and willingness to work. The lender can then compare, from his or her own experience in lending money to other businesses, the relative strengths of your proposal.

2.   Organizational structure

If you are going into business with more than one person (either in a partnership or with an incorporated company), set out the organizational structure on an organization chart listing the title of each major owner and stating the role that each will play in helping run the operation. Also, if one of the owners has some particular expertise (for example, has one of them operated a similar type of restaurant before?), be sure to explain this since it adds weight and credibility to your proposal and can help influence a potential lender to advance you any required funds.

3.   Personal financial information

If you do not have a previous business track record, the lender will probably ask for personal financial information about you and any other owners. This shows the lender what financial support you can fall back on if the restaurant is not immediately successful and requires further owner investment. A sample personal financial information form is illustrated in Sample #6.

A key figure in this form is the difference between assets and liabilities, often referred to as net worth. If you are going into business with one or more partners, each of them would normally be required to produce a net worth statement.

4.   References

You need to provide references, both personal and business. If you have dealt with other banks previously, references from them can be helpful, including details of any previous or present loans outstanding with those banks. The names of your accountant and lawyer are also useful for references.

5.   Financial statements

Financial statement projections are required for the next 12 months with detailed calculations showing, in particular, how total annual sales are calculated and what the operating costs are projected to be. Forecast cash flow projections, month by month for the next year, are also required. The lender is interested in how your business is expected to do and, most important, its ability to repay any loans according to projected cash flow.

In particular, the lender is looking for potential problems indicated by your financial statements. These problems could be matters such as proposing to extend too much credit, too high an inventory in relation to sales, too high a proposed dividend payout or owner cash withdrawals, a possible serious decline in sales in poor economic times, or too much investment in fixed assets in relation to sales.

The amount of your investment or equity in the business is important. Banks and other lending institutions do not

SAMPLE #6
PERSONAL FINANCIAL INFORMATION FORM

TO: **BIG BANK**

(USE A SEPARATE PAGE FOR DETAILS IF SPACE INSUFFICIENT IN ANY AREA)

TRANSIT	BRANCH	DATE

LAST NAME	FIRST NAME	INITIAL	MR MRS

ADDRESS	APT. NO.	HOME TELEPHONE	BUSINESS TELEPHONE	IF RESIDENCE OWNED, DESCRIBE: [ ] DETACHED [ ] SEMI [ ] TOWN HOUSE [ ] CONDOMINIUM
	POSTAL CODE	BIRTHPLACE		YEAR PURCH	PRESENT VALUE	TAXES PAID	MONTHLY PAYMENTS (P.I.T.) $

MARITAL STATUS: [ ] SINGLE [ ] DIVORCED [ ] MARRIED [ ] SEPARATED	SPOUSE FIRST NAME	NO. DEPENDENTS	MORTGAGES OWING TO	MATURES	PRESENT AMOUNT
DATE OF BIRTH DAY MONTH YEAR					FIRE INSURANCE $

AT PRESENT ADDRESS FOR _____ YEARS	PREVIOUS ADDRESS IF AT ABOVE LESS THAN 2 YEARS	REGISTERED OWNER(S)
[ ] OWN [ ] RENT $ _____ PER MONTH		OTHER PROPERTY OWNED

MTGE AMT $
NET EQUITY $

EMPLOYMENT AND INCOME

FINANCIAL POSITION SUMMARY

EMPLOYER (NAME AND ADDRESS)	OCCUPATION	HOW LONG	GROSS ANNUAL EARNINGS $	OTHER FAMILY INCOME $
PREVIOUS EMPLOYER (IF WITH ABOVE LESS THAN 2 YEARS)	OCCUPATION	HOW LONG	GROSS ANNUAL EARNINGS $	SOURCE:
SPOUSE NOW EMPLOYED BY (NAME AND ADDRESS)	OCCUPATION	HOW LONG	GROSS ANNUAL EARNINGS $	

ASSETS

BANK ACCOUNTS	$
REAL ESTATE	
STOCKS AND BONDS	
LIFE INSURANCE, ETC. (CASH VALUE)	
CAR YEAR MAKE MODEL	
OTHER	

TOTAL ASSETS $

ACCOUNTS AT	[ ] LOCATION OF OTHER ACCOUNTS OR [ ] PREVIOUS BANK IF NEW ACCOUNT
THIS BRANCH	

NAME AND ADDRESS OF NEAREST RELATIVE NOT LIVING WITH ME/US.	TELEPHONE	RELATIONSHIP

INVESTMENTS (STOCKS, BONDS, TERM DEPOSITS, LIFE INSURANCE)

TYPE	COMPANY/ISSUER	FACE VALUE/UNITS	MARKET VALUE	IF ASSIGNED, WHO TO?

LIABILITIES

INSTALLMENT ACCOUNTS/DEBTS (AS SHOWN)	$
AMOUNT OF MORTGAGES OWING (AS ABOVE)	
INCOME TAXES OWING	
REAL ESTATE TAXES	
OTHER	

TOTAL LIABILITIES $

NET WORTH $

INSTALLMENT ACCOUNTS/DEBTS OWING

	NAME/ACCOUNT NUMBER	PURPOSE	OWING SINCE	ORIGINAL AMOUNT	NOW OWING	MONTHLY PAYMENT
OWING TO THIS OR OTHER BANKS FINANCE COMPANIES OR CREDIT UNIONS				$	$	$
CHARGE ACCOUNTS						
CHARGEX/VISA						

TOTAL

IF NEW LOAN ACCOUNT, RECORD IDENTIFICATION DETAILS (e.g. DRIVERS LICENCE NUMBER)

THE ABOVE INFORMATION IS PROVIDED TO THE BANK AS A FCTUAL STATEMENT OF MY AFFAIRS. YOU MAY AT ANY TIME OBTAIN INFORMATION ABOUT ME FROM MY EMPLOYER, ANY CREDIT BUREAU OR ANY OTHER PERSON IN CONNECTION WITH ANY OF MY DEALINGS WITH YOU. IN ADDITION, YOU MAY DISCLOSE INFORMATION AND DOCUMENTS RELATING TO MY CREDIT HISTORY WITH YOU TO ANY CREDIT BUREAU, TO ANY PERSON WITH WHOM I HAVE OR PROPOSE TO HAVE FINANCIAL DEALINGS, OR IF YOU BELIEVE THAT THE DISCLOSURE IS REQUIRED BY LAW.

_____ SIGNATURE

_____ SIGNATURE

finance 100% of the money needed by a new business. You have to put some of your own money in — as much as 25% of the total cash required. If you are not prepared to risk your own money, why should the bank risk its funds?

6. Security offered

The prospective lender wants details of the security offered for any loan. This includes a description of the assets (land, building, equipment, and fixtures). If you can offer personal security (house, stocks, bonds, life insurance, and similar items) this too should be listed.

A recent appraisal, (if you have one) on the land and/or building (if you plan to buy them) is useful since it indicates what the property is worth. If the land and/or building are not owned, your lease agreement might be the security offered. In such a case, provide a copy of the lease agreement along with a statement from the lessor showing that all rent payments already made (if any) have been made promptly.

7. Insurance policies

The lender wants to know if the business is adequately insured against losses and liabilities and, in each case, who the beneficiaries are. Therefore, make copies of insurance policies available to the lender.

8. Other considerations

The importance of careful preparation of all the paperwork outlined above cannot be overstressed. The manner in which this information is professionally prepared and presented to a potential lender will go a long way toward ensuring that the required funds will be obtained.

In calculations of sales and expenses, accuracy is critical. Careless errors are made in overestimating revenue or underestimating expenses (thus producing a "padded" profit amount) will damage your credibility. The chances of obtaining borrowed funds will be considerably decreased. For this reason, professional help from an accountant may be necessary.

The documentation suggested above includes the papers most likely to be required by a lender, but it might also be a good idea to contact specific potential lenders to determine what information they would like to have. This ensures that you don't waste time putting together a report that is either far too detailed for a lender's purposes or that fails to include some specific item the lender wants.

When seeking financing, it is a good idea to make appointments in a businesslike way with each potential lender. That is more likely to portray the image of a professional business operator than by just simply walking in the door and asking for money.

A example of a financing proposal is shown in Sample #7.

b. LENDING DECISIONS

When you are applying for funds, there are two possibilities: the funding will be approved or denied.

1. Funding approved

If a request for financing is approved, find out everything you need to know about the conditions, terms, payment methods, interest rates, security requirements, and if there are any front-end charges or fees to be paid. No commitment to accept the financing should be made until all this information is provided and understood, and its impact on the proposed business purchase analyzed.

If financing is approved with certain conditions, determine if these conditions are severe enough to restrict the operating standards desired. Will the conditions commit you to more than was intended, or are they normal financing requirements that were simply overlooked?

Once a final commitment is arranged, plan to provide the lender with copies of future financial statements. Frequently this will be one of the requirements for obtaining funding. Even if it is not, it will provide the lender with progress reports about the restaurant and will be helpful to the lender in processing future applications for further financing.

2. Funding denied

If a request for funding is not approved, find out why. Use the lender's experience to advantage. He or she will have a reason for not providing the financing. For example, the lender might be able to see that, with the financial plan you have proposed, your restaurant will run into a shortage of working capital. This is one of the common reasons for restaurant failure.

Once a restaurant is in trouble because of a shortage of working capital, it is often difficult to obtain additional working capital assistance. A potential lender may well be able to point this out as a problem with your financing plan. It is far preferable to ask for additional funds to strengthen working capital at the outset.

If there is something else wrong with the financing proposal, see if it can be corrected and then reapply. If not, use this knowledge when approaching other potential lenders.

Once you have exhausted most normal channels of financing, such as banks, commercial finance companies, consumer finance companies, and credit unions, you can pursue the following possible sources of money.

c. SMALL BUSINESS ADMINISTRATION (U.S.)

In the U.S., if all else fails, you might consider the U.S. Small Business Administration (SBA). It is responsible for assisting entrepreneurs and its functions include, among others, finance and investment.

The SBA is organized into 10 regions and each region is subdivided, providing district or branch office in many population centers. As the lender of final resort, the SBA tries not to compete with or replace the private banking system but to supplement it.

SBA guidelines defining who qualifies for small business assistance vary, depending on the general classification of the enterprise. At present, the eligibility of a business is measured by sales volume or revenue. For example, the upper limit is $14.5 million per year for a retail/service business such as a restaurant.

Loans made by SBA generally mature in 10 years or less for fixtures and equipment, and are repaid in equal monthly installments of principal and interest, although this time period may be extended to 25 years where the purchase of land and/or a building are concerned.

Working capital loans can be made for periods up to seven years. Regardless of the loan term, the loan may be repaid at any time prior to maturity without penalty.

Since the SBA's regulations sometimes change, you should verify current conditions by contacting your nearest branch of the SBA (listed in your telephone directory under U.S. Government) or write:

Small Business Administration
Washington, D.C. 20416

d. GOVERNMENT FINANCING IN CANADA

The Small Businesses Loans Act (SBLA) will lend up to $250,000 to a small business whose annual gross revenue is not over $5 million. The floating interest rate cannot exceed 1.75% over the prime lending rate and the maximum term is 10 years.

There will be a one-time front-end fee of 2% of the loan the bank must collect and pay to the federal government. The fee may be charged to the borrower and may be added to the amount of the loan.

Restaurants are eligible for funding under the SBLA as long as the loan is not for working capital requirements or to repay an existing loan.

All chartered banks and Alberta Treasury Branches are authorized to make loans under the SBLA. In addition, loans may be made by credit unions, caisses populaires, or other cooperative societies, trust companies, loan companies, and insurance companies, which have applied and have been designated as lenders under the act.

Therefore, if all the other sources fail, talk to your own banker or other lender about the SBLA, and obtain a credit application. If you want further information about SBLA write to:

Industry, Science and Technology Canada
SBA Branch
C.D. Howe Building
8th Floor
235 Queen Street
Ottawa, Ontario
K1A 0H5

In Canada, you should also be aware of the Federal Business Development Bank, or FBDB. This lender is sometimes referred to as the lender of last resort and was established by the government especially to help those companies that could not obtain financing elsewhere.

If your funding application has been turned down by other financial institutions, you may apply to the FBDB. To obtain FBDB financing, the amount of your investment in the restaurant must generally be sufficient to ensure that you are committed to it and that the restaurant may reasonably be expected to succeed.

Financing from the FBDB can range from a few thousand to $100,000. Not many loans are made in excess of that amount. The amount that can be borrowed for a specific purpose depends on your ability to satisfy the bank's general requirements.

The FBDB also offers management counselling, management training, and other business information services including CASE (Counselling Assistance for Small Enterprise). CASE helps owners and managers of small businesses improve their methods of doing business. To be eligible, you can already be established, or about to be established, in business in Canada. One restriction is that you must not have more than 75 full-time employees. There is also a nominal daily charge for this service. If you wish to pursue this, contact your local branch of the FBDB, or write to:

Federal Business Development Bank
P.O. Box 335
Stock Exchange Tower Station
Montreal, Quebec
H4Z 1L4

Personal resume

Name	Resta Rawnt
Address	#1201 - 1855 Columbia Anytown
Telephone	986-5432
Personal	Born September 15, 1961 Marital status: single
Education	Completed high school in Anytown Received Hotel/Restaurant Management diploma at Community College, Anytown, 1980 Since then I have taken some other specialized night courses in marketing and public relations at the College.
Employment/ business experience	Worked as waitress part time while going to high school and attending college. From 1980 to 1987 worked in various restaurants as waitress, cashier and hostess. Since 1987 have been the manager of the Ritz Restaurant in Anytown. The present owner of the Ritz Restaurant assumed ownership four years ago when the restaurant was losing money. During this period, while I was manager, this situation was turned around and for the past three years the restaurant has made a steady annual profit.

Restaurant plan

My plan is to start a restaurant in the shortly to be opened National Bank Building in Anytown.

I shall be renting 1,000 square feet of space on the ground floor of that building for a 75-seat restaurant.

My marketing research indicates that there should be a steady clientele from the other businesses in the tower and from shoppers in the adjacent mall.

The restaurant will be open 6 days a week from 7:30 a.m. until 6 p.m.

The income statements appended show that sales are projected at $33,000 a month, and profit $2,500 a month. The monthly payroll expense of $10,400 includes a salary of $2,000 that I plan to pay myself.

Personal financial information

This personal financial information is relevant as at October 31, 199-.

ASSETS	
Bank accounts	
— Checking	$ 300
— Savings	2,200
Government bonds	15,000
Stocks — market value	3,800
Automobile	2,700
Real estate — condominium	$105,000
Total assets	$129,000
LIABILITIES	
Accounts payable — charge accounts	$ 700
Mortgage payable (condominium)	79,000
Installment account (auto)	2,200
Other liabilities	0
Total liabilities	$ 81,900
NET WORTH	$ 47,100

References

Banks:

1. National Bank
   Main Branch
   Anytown
   (checking account #7-456890 and savings account 64-102076)

2. Savers Credit Union
   Main Branch
   Anytown   (mortgage records)

Lawyer:

Sol Soliciter
Beagle, Legal, & Iciter
#107 - 455 Humber St.
Anytown
(434-5736)

Accountant:

Charlene Counter
Counter & Total
#512 - 1040 Broadway
Anytown
(732-1611)

Financial projections

Total financing cost will be:

Inventory and other working capital	$ 5,000
Equipment, furniture and fixtures	85,000
Total	$90,000

The plan for financing this $90,000 investment is:

Personal savings (equity investment) from cash and by selling stocks and bonds	$18,000
Bank loan for balance	72,000
Total	$90,000

The bank loan will be repayable in equal monthly installments of principal and interest over three years. Given current interest rates the monthly total repayment amount for principal and interest is calculated to be $2,500.

Income statement

The forecast monthly income statement is as follows:

Sales:		
Food	$30,000	
Beverage	3,000	
		$33,000
Cost of sales:		
Food	$12,000	
Beverage	900	
		12,900
Gross profit		$20,100
Expenses:		
Payroll	$10,400	
Employee benefits	2,100	
Laundry	200	
China, glass, silver	100	
Supplies	200	
Miscellaneous	200	
Advertising	200	
Utilities	300	
Management salary	1,800	
Office	500	
Rent	600	
Insurance	100	
Interest	700	
Depreciation	200	
		$17,600
Net profit		$ 2,500

Cash flow

The monthly cash flow from the business will be:

Monthly net profit	$ 2,500
Add back depreciation	200
	$ 2,700
Deduct principal repayments	1,900
Net cash flow	$ 800

This net cash flow shows a relatively high margin of safety.

Security offered

The following security is offered:

1.   Personal guarantee

2.   Chattel mortgage on furniture and equipment.

3.   Lease agreement. I have discussed the lease with the landlord who agrees that, if financing can be acquired, he would be prepared to offer a lease for a five-year period starting January 1, 199-, with a further five-year renewal option. Rent payments will be $600 a month, with rent tied to the CPI for inflationary purposes at the start of each new year. The landlord can be contacted to confirm this arrangement:

Mr. John Lessor
Ipso Investments
#307 - 4551 Main St.
Anytown
(Tel. 684-4685)

4.   Additional security can be offered, if necessary, by way of a second mortgage (trust deed) on the condominium.

14
FRANCHISING

You might want to consider taking over an existing franchise business, or buying into a franchising system and opening up a new franchised outlet. Franchising as a means for the independent entrepreneur to go into business has been booming for the last 20 years and there appears to be no immediate letup in sight.

You only need to look at popular business journals and newspaper business sections or even in the business opportunities section of newspaper classified advertising to see the many references made to franchised restaurants.

a. A DEFINITION OF FRANCHISING

No commonly accepted definition of franchising can be applied in all cases. However, in general terms, it is a method of distribution or marketing in which a company (the franchisor) grants by contract to an individual or another company (the franchisee) the right to carry on a business in a prescribed way in a particular location for a specified period.

The franchisee may be allowed to operate only one establishment, or may be given an area in which a number of franchised outlets may be operated. That area could be a city, a state or province, a major portion of the country, or indeed the whole country.

For the services that it provides, the franchisor receives a fee, or royalty, usually based on gross sales, or else a fixed fee (for example, a flat monthly or annual amount). In addition, you, as the franchisee, usually have to pay a share of local, regional, or national advertising costs. Again, this advertising cost is usually a percentage of sales revenue. The fees and other costs are generally payable monthly.

For what you pay as a franchisee, you may receive business advice and counsel, financial aid (direct or indirect), market research, lease negotiation, site evaluation, building plans, training programs, national advertising, an accounting system, and an established and widely recognized name and image.

Although you must provide, or arrange for, most of the financing required, the franchisor may provide some of this initial capital. In such cases, the monthly fee will probably include an extra amount to pay back this franchisor financing, with interest.

b. ADVANTAGES TO THE INDIVIDUAL FRANCHISEE

Some of the major advantages of taking the franchise route into the restaurant business are:

(a) It is possible to start up as a generally independent entrepreneur but with the support of an established parent company: the franchisor. The franchisor may provide you with assistance in such matters as obtaining financing, site selection, building construction supervision, employee training, and support during the difficult break-in period subsequent to opening.

(b) As a franchisee, you have the opportunity to buy into an established concept, although this, by itself, is no guarantee that you will succeed. However, the risk of failure is generally reduced. Statistics show that the independent entrepreneur opening a small business only has a 20% to 30% chance of surviving the first few critical years. For franchisees, similar statistics show there is an 80% chance of success.

(c) You have the ongoing backup of the franchisor, who can provide assistance and help solve problems since he or she can afford to hire specialists in the head office in such areas as cost control, marketing and sales, and research and development.

(d) The franchisor can provide the potential for local, regional, or even national advertising (albeit at a cost to you).

(e) You have access to credit that you may not otherwise have. Banks and similar lending institutions are usually more willing to lend money to a restaurateur who has the backing of a successful franchisor than they would to the completely independent entrepreneur.

(f) You may be able to purchase supplies at a reduced cost since the franchisor can purchase in bulk and pass the savings on to the franchisees (as much as 3% to 6% on costs may be saved this way).

(g) You may find an opportunity to take over a turnkey franchise operation. A turnkey operation is one where the franchisor provides you with a completely set up franchise. The franchisor assists in obtaining financing; evaluating, selecting, and acquiring the site; constructing and equipping the premises; training you and your staff; providing "startup" assistance; purchasing the initial inventory; providing management and accounting reporting systems; providing advertising, public rela-

tions, and marketing services; and, after opening, providing ongoing supervision and guidance. In other words, about all you have to do is turn the key in the door and you're in business.

(h) If you are taking over a franchised restaurant, or starting a new one with a franchising company, you may be able to take advantage of a master lease. In this situation, the franchising company becomes the landlord's tenant but is allowed to sublease the operation to you. Because the franchising company is a good risk, the landlord may charge a lower rent than if you rented directly. The rent saving is then split in an agreed fashion between the franchisor and you, the franchisee.

(i) Finally, franchising offers many of the advantages of an integrated chain business (without some of the disadvantages) because of the voluntary nature of the contract rather than central ownership.

c. DISADVANTAGES TO THE INDIVIDUAL FRANCHISEE

Just as you must consider the advantages of the franchised form of business, so must you also consider the disadvantages.

(a) The cost of the services provided by the franchisor come off the top of your sales revenue and could add up to 10% or more of that revenue.

(b) Even though the franchise arrangement allows you to start a restaurant that you might otherwise only be able to begin with difficulty, you will have some loss of freedom since the franchisor's standards have to be adhered to, and you may have limited scope for individual personal initiative.

(c) In some cases, the markup that the franchisor adds to the products that you must buy from him or her can increase your operating costs, particularly if an equally good product could be purchased locally at a lower cost.

(d) Experience shows that you run some risk of not achieving the sales potential, and thus the profit, that the franchisor stated was possible when selling the franchise.

(e) If the franchisor operates from a jurisdiction other than the one in which you have the franchise, and his or her obligations are not fulfilled, it can be difficult, if not impossible, to seek redress.

d. BEFORE PROCEEDING

Do not buy into a franchise based on the lure of quick profits, minimum effort, low initial investment, and freedom to be your own boss. Too many entrepreneurs, in evaluating a franchise, disregard any warning lights, push aside sensible (generally negative) advice, and fail to completely examine the franchisor or the contract, even when the franchisor suggests that this be done.

Some franchisees end up being very well off, but by far the majority find themselves working harder than they anticipated under contract arrangements that may seem harsh or restrictive since they do not provide the anticipated return on investment. Some of these entrepreneurs fail, since they expected too much from too little effort on their part.

If you would like further information on franchising, see *Franchising in the U.S.* or *Franchising in Canada*, two other titles in the Self-Counsel Series.

In any case, do not sign a franchise contract until you have carefully investigated the franchisor and have had a lawyer check the contract for you.

15
PURCHASING

At the time that you decide to purchase your initial inventory for your restaurant a cost is incurred. Every time you reorder to replenish that inventory, further costs are incurred. Therefore, to minimize these costs, attention should be paid to the purchasing function.

Larger restaurants and chains frequently have separate purchasing departments on their payroll with one or more employees solely involved in purchasing. Effective purchasing usually reduces overall costs. To illustrate, consider a restaurant in the following situation:

Sales	$1,000,000
Cost of sales	400,000
Other costs	550,000
Net profit	$ 50,000

If the above restaurant could save ½ of 1% through more effective purchasing, it would be $20,000 (½% x $400,000). Assuming no other costs change, profit would thus increase from $50,000 to $70,000 — an increase in profit of 40%!

The purpose of purchasing, whether carried out by you or someone you delegate, is to make sure needed inventory and other supplies and services are available in appropriate quantities, at the right price, and at a minimum cost to meet desired standards.

The person responsible for purchasing, regardless of the size of restaurant, can benefit from applying some of the basic purchasing practices and procedures discussed in this chapter. By following these procedures you can avoid purchasing pitfalls such as panic buying, over- or short-purchasing, buying by price rather than by a combination of quality and price, pressure buying, or, what is probably quite common, "satisfied buying." Satisfied buying means the purchaser assumes no improvements in either quality or price can be achieved.

a. THE PURCHASING CYCLE

There are a number of steps in the purchasing cycle. The major ones are:

(a) Recognizing the need to purchase goods

(b) Preparing specifications, if necessary

(c) Selecting a supplier

(d) Receiving the goods

(e) Storing the goods

1. Recognizing the need

In many small restaurants the owner does all the purchasing. In a larger restaurant, this task may be delegated to others, such as the chef or the dining room manager, or even to a separate purchasing department in a very large restaurant.

In a small restaurant, as the owner/operator, you will know best what does and does not sell, what you have in inventory, market conditions and prices, and any special items you can add to your menu. You are in the best position to recognize the need to purchase specific goods.

2. Preparing specifications

Whenever practical, you should prepare purchasing specifications for major items, or for items that are being ordered for the first time. A specification is simply a carefully written description of the items desired. It includes, for example, the quality of seafood you want or the way you want the steaks cut.

Specifications should be prepared so that one copy can be sent to each potential supplier and copies distributed to appropriate employees, such as the person responsible for receiving the goods.

The language of the specifications must be sufficiently precise so there is no misunderstanding between you and the supplier. However, this does not mean that, once prepared, specifications cannot be changed. Indeed, as market conditions, or the needs of your restaurant change, new sets of specifications should be prepared.

The main advantages of specifications are that they —

(a) require those who prepare them to think carefully and document exactly what their product requirements are,

(b) leave no doubt in suppliers' minds about what they are quoting on, thus reducing or eliminating misunderstandings between supplier and you,

(c) eliminate, for frequently purchased items, the time that would otherwise have to be spent repeating descriptions over the telephone, or directly to salespeople, each time the good or product is needed,

(d) permit competitive bidding, and

(e) allow the person responsible for receiving to check the quality of delivered goods against a written description of the quality desired.

3. **Selecting suppliers**

The important consideration in selecting final suppliers is to contact as many of them as is practical to ensure that enough quotations are received so that the right quality of product is purchased at the lowest possible price.

A minimum of three quotations is recommended for each separate product or service to ensure that competitive pricing prevails. These quotations may be in writing or given over the telephone.

You should buy the items you need that have the quality you want at the lowest cost. This does not mean always buying at the lowest price since the lowest price may mean poor quality. Also, the "yield" of an item may be important. For example, a cut of meat from one supplier may be lower priced than from a second. However, when trimmed with fat removed, the second supplier's price may in fact be lower because of the higher yield.

Similarly, canned vegetables and fruit, when drained of liquid may yield substantially different weights. You should test your products from time to time to make sure you are benefitting from the lowest price.

When you order items, it is a good idea to use a market quotation sheet such as the one in Sample #8. The items circled are the ones ordered. This sheet can be helpful when you are receiving so you know what is to be delivered from which suppliers and at what prices.

For certain products you may want to purchase from farmers' markets. They are a useful source of fresh produce for small restaurants. They are seldom used by large restaurants that have to buy in relatively large quantities.

Markets offer such items as fresh fruit and vegetables, fish, eggs, poultry, meat, smoked meat, and dairy products. They are usually open seven days a week, often for extended hours. Prices may be lower, and products fresher than from other suppliers, but, to be sure, you must be familiar with local prices and qualities from other sources. Prices can be lower because the individual producers/sellers are able to bypass wholesale distributors.

As an alternative, you might also consider using your local supermarket for food and other supplies. The main advantage of this source is that virtually all products used by most small restaurants are available in one location. Supermarkets also offer the convenience of seven-day-a-week opening, which means products required can be purchased daily. This reduces the need to carry an inventory on site, reduces loss from spoilage, and allows better cost control. Because they have tremendous buying power, supermarkets sometimes have lower prices than other suppliers. They also tend to have excellent and reliable quality control systems.

Another advantage of both farmers' markets and supermarkets is that you have to pay cash, thus reducing the problems that can occur when you receive credit from a supplier, fail to pay bills on time, then begin to have cash flow problems.

However, despite lower prices and/or better quality, there may be a disadvantage for even a very small restaurant in purchasing from farmers' markets or supermarkets. To the cost of the product must be added the cost of providing your own transportation (the cost of operating the vehicle and the cost of a person's time to pick up the needed products).

For example, if the chef does farmers' market or supermarket purchasing for a small restaurant, would the time not be better spent supervising today's kitchen production rather than "shopping"?

4. Receiving goods

The next step in the purchasing cycle is receiving the goods. Tell suppliers your

SAMPLE #8
MARKET QUOTATION SHEET

		Date_____			
Item	**Quantity required**	**Suppliers**			
CHEESE		Vintange	Louie	ABC	
American	10 kg	(5.10)	5.40	5.18	
Bel Paese	2 kg	7.19	8.30	(7.10)	
Camembert	5 kg	12.10	(11.15)	12.10	
Cheddar, Mild	10 kg	6.10	(5.95)	6.04	
Cheddar, Medium	10 kg	6.30	6.40	(6.18)	
Cheddar, Strong	10 kg	6.70	(6.60)	6.75	
Cottage	8 kg	(3.71)	3.95	3.80	

standard receiving hours so they can schedule deliveries when you, or your delegates, are there.

In all cases where specifications have been prepared, you should have a copy on hand during the receiving process so that delivered goods can be checked against the specifications. In particular, quantities received should be checked against quantities ordered and invoiced.

When items are purchased by weight, weighing scales of an appropriate type should be provided so that weights can be verified against invoiced weights.

Finally, prices on invoices should be checked against the quotation references (see Sample #8). Quality control tests may need to be performed to ensure that the quality of delivered items meets the specifications. Any damage to delivered goods should be reported immediately to the supplier for adjustment.

All delivery slips (or invoices if invoices accompany the deliveries) should be stamped, and the stamp should be initialled in the appropriate spots to indicate that all the required checking has been completed. A typical receiving stamp is illustrated in Sample #9.

If goods are short-shipped, or returned to the supplier for any reason, it is a good idea to fill in a credit memo and have the delivery driver sign it. This is your proof that the goods should not be paid for and ensures that the supplier will issue an appropriate credit invoice. A sample credit memo is illustrated in Sample #10.

5. Storing goods

The last step in the purchasing cycle is the storage of goods until they are needed. As soon as possible after receiving, put goods into their proper storage areas. There are three basic types of storage area required by most restaurants: dry storage, refrigerated storage, and freezer storage.

Dry storage can be used for both food and alcoholic beverages, or you could have a separate dry storage area for each of these. The temperature should not be too warm since warmth encourages bacteria that can lead to food spoilage. For the same reason, the humidity of your dry storage should be kept as low as possible. Dry storage needs to be well ventilated, with adequate sturdy shelving so that goods are not piled on top of each other.

Refrigerated storage should be kept at different temperatures for different products. If you can afford the luxury of separated refrigerated areas, use these temperature ranges:

Meat	32° to 36°F or 0° to 2°C
Fruit and vegetables	35° to 45°F or 2° to 7°C
Dairy products	38° to 46°F or 3° to 8°C

If you only have one refrigerated area, you will have to compromise and keep the temperature in the 35° to 40°F (2° to 5°C) range.

The temperature of your freezer area should, of course, be kept below freezing.

Proper attention paid to storage areas is suggested not only to minimize your losses, but also for reasons of sanitation. Before opening your restaurant, ask your local health authorities what specific requirements they have for your locale. You should do this not only to conform to these requirements, but also to prevent sanitation problems that could lead to possible food poisoning, lawsuits, or even your restaurant's closure.

b. INVENTORY CONTROL

You need to have some control over items in storage, or in inventory. For refrigerated and freezer items, this may be difficult since there may be two or more people working in food preparation who must have constant easy access to these items.

SAMPLE #9
RECEIVING STAMP

RECEIVING STAMP

Date received _____

Quantity checked by _____

Quality checked by _____

Prices checked by _____

Listed on receiving report by _____

SAMPLE #10
CREDIT MEMORANDUM

CREDIT MEMORANDUM

Supplier_____Date_____

Please issue a credit memorandum for the following:

Quantity	Item description	Unit cost	Total

Reason for request for credit:

Delivery driver's signature_____

96

Supervision is about the only method of control for those types of food items.

For goods in dry storage (both food and alcoholic beverages), a system of perpetual inventory cards and requisitions may be useful to you as a control system.

The objectives in control are to minimize losses, avoid running out of items, and minimize the investment or money tied up in inventory. Funds needlessly tied up in inventory are not earning a profit (in fact, carrying an inventory costs money). If you left money in the bank rather than putting it into inventory it would be earning a profit — the interest rate paid to you by the bank. In other words, the problem is one of both physical and financial control of your inventory.

1. Perpetual inventory cards

One good way to keep track of the inventory you have on hand in your dry goods storeroom is to use a system of perpetual inventory cards.

An individual card is required for each type of item carried in inventory. A sample card is illustrated in Sample #11. The "In" column figures are taken from the invoices delivered with the goods. The figures in the "Out" column are for items that have been taken out of the storeroom.

2. Requisitions

Larger restaurants use requisitions so that those authorized to receive items from the storeroom will record their requests on this form. A typical requisition is illustrated in Sample #12.

These requisitions are prepared in advance by employees and then presented to the person responsible for the storeroom. In a small restaurant, this person is usually the owner or manager who issues items during restricted hours. The rest of the time the storeroom is kept locked. Larger restaurants may need a full-time storekeeper.

A small restaurant might even want to completely do away with requisitions. In such a case, a simple sheet on which all items removed each day are recorded can be used. Employees are simply instructed to record on this sheet, kept near the storeroom door, any items taken from the storeroom. At the end of the day, the requisitioned goods figures are recorded in the "Out" column of the appropriate perpetual inventory cards.

3. Quantity control

Obviously, if all "In" and "Out" figures are properly recorded on the cards , the "Balance" figure on the card will agree with the actual count of the item on the shelf or rack. Thus the cards can be useful in inventory control.

The cards also help ensure that items are not overstocked or understocked since they can show the maximum inventory for each individual item and the minimum point to which that stock level can fall before the item needs to be reordered.

Instead of counting the items actually in stock, you only have to go through each of the cards in turn once a week, or however frequently it is practical to reorder, and list all items for which the "Balance" figure is at or close to the minimum point. Then order the quantity required to bring the inventory up to par.

Note that the cards can also be designed to carry the names and telephone numbers of suggested suppliers.

4. Inventory turnover

Another useful inventory control technique is that of inventory turnover. Calculating inventory turnover will show you in a general way whether you have too little or too much money tied up in inventory.

Inventory turnover for a month is calculated as follows:

$$\frac{\text{Cost of goods sold}}{\text{Average inventory}}$$

SAMPLE #11
PERPETUAL INVENTORY CARD

PERPETUAL INVENTORY CARD

Item __Tomatoes, canned #10 size__   Supplier __Savage__   Tel. No. __683-0202__

Minimum __1 case of 6 cans__   Supplier __Louie__   Tel. No. __497-6840__

Maximum __5 cases of 6 cans__   Supplier __CANPAK__   Tel. No. __680-1219__

Date	In	Out	Balance forward 6 cans	Item cost information
Nov 11	24		30	$1.83 per can
Nov 12		3	27	

Cost of goods sold is:

Beginning of month inventory +
Purchases for month -
End of month
inventory

Average inventory is:

(Beginning inventory +
Ending inventory) divided by 2

Using the following figures:

Beginning inventory $2,000
Purchases for month $8,500
Ending inventory $3,000

The inventory turnover would be:

$$\frac{\$2,000 + \$8,500 - \$3,000}{(\$2,000 + \$3,000) \div 2} = \frac{\$7,500}{\$2,500} = 3.0$$

Generally, the higher the turnover rate, the lower the amount of money invested in inventory, and vice versa. The inventory turnover rate can vary widely from one type of restaurant to another, and even for restaurants of the same type.

Generally, however, the inventory turnover figure for food is between two and four times a month, and for liquor between one-half and one time a month.

c. PURCHASE DISCOUNTS

Whenever a purchase discount is offered, you should consider the benefit of taking it. For example, suppose the terms are 2/10, net 60. On a $5,000 purchase paid within 10 days, this would save $100 (2% x $5,000). This can amount to a considerable sum if it is made on all similar purchases during a year. However, in the example given, you may have to borrow the money ($4,900) in order to make the payment within 10 days. If the money were borrowed for 50 days (60 days less 10 days) at a 10% interest rate, the interest expense would be:

$$\frac{\$4,900 \times 50 \text{ days} \times 10\%}{365 \text{ days}} = \$67.12$$

In this case, it would be advantageous to borrow the money since the discount saving of $100 is greater than the interest expense of $67.12.

SAMPLE #12
REQUISITION

REQUISITION		
Department _____ Date _____		
Quantity	Size	Item description
Authorized signature _____		

16
FOOD, LIQUOR, AND LABOR COST CONTROL

One of the major problems that restaurateurs face in cost control is the perishable nature of food. Perishability is a problem from the moment of receiving through storage, preparation, production, and service.

As well as "normal" perishability (such things as frozen foods thawed for too long and vegetables and fruit becoming bruised), there is the "perishability" resulting from employee theft.

Control over your food losses is established through "food cost" control, or the ratio of food cost expense to sales. You must therefore establish a system that allows you to know what your food cost should be and then measure how the actual cost compares with that. If you don't know what your food cost should be, you are operating completely blind.

The following are recommended steps in establishing a standard control system:

(a) Establish standard recipes and portion sizes

(b) Calculate menu item costs

(c) Set your selling prices

(d) Evaluate your results

a. ESTABLISH STANDARD RECIPES AND PORTION SIZES

Standard recipes need to be prepared for each of your menu items. The standard recipe is a written formula detailing the quantity of each ingredient required in that menu item to produce the quantity and quality you want.

The recipe should describe the cooking procedure and temperature, where necessary, since temperature can affect the shrinkage, quality, and end cost of the menu item. Recipes should define the portion size to be served (e.g., 2 ounces of shrimp in a seafood cocktail).

Your cooking employees must be trained to follow these recipes and portion sizes, not only for cost control reasons but also to ensure that customers receive a consistent size and quality.

Portion scales should be provided where they are needed, such as in weighing sliced meat, or seafood for a cocktail. These scales do not need to be used for measuring each portion, but for checking from time to time that there is no deviation from standard portions. Measuring devices, such as ladles, scoops, or spoons, or individual cooking utensils (such as casserole dishes), should be used.

If you allow employees to use their own judgment about portion sizes, you will have no control. You need to spot check from time to time to see that standard recipes and portion sizes are being followed by your employees. A typical standard recipe form is illustrated in Sample #13.

b. CALCULATE MENU ITEM COSTS

The next step is to calculate menu item costs. This is simply a question of multiplying the quantity of each ingredient used in that menu item by its cost as shown on Sample #13.

If ingredient costs change drastically, you must recalculate this cost. Alternatively, to compensate you could make some change in the portion size or selling price so that the relationship between cost and selling price remains the same.

As long as you have only a limited number of items on your menu, these cost calculations can easily be done by hand. If your menu is long, and the number of ingredients you use runs into the hundreds, you can use software programs that are now available for a home or microcomputer. They automatically recalculate your menu item costs when you enter the new ingredient cost(s).

c. SET YOUR SELLING PRICES

When you know what your cost is for each menu item, you can then establish a selling price.

Suppose you want to have a food cost percent, or cost of sales, of 40%. You simply take the cost of a menu item, multiply it by 100 and divide by 40. For example, if your standard recipe is $2.00, then the selling price to give you a 40% food cost is:

$$\$2.00 \ x \frac{100}{40} = \$5.00$$

However, it may not be practical to mark up every item by the same percentage. When you set your menu prices, you must keep in mind other factors such as who your customers are, what they are prepared to pay, and what your competition may be charging for similar menu items.

You then have to juggle a little bit. If you want an overall 40% food cost, some menu items might be costed at 45% or 50% and others at 30% or 35% — so that the overall average works out to your desired standard.

There is nothing magic abut the 40% overall food cost used above. Some restaurants operate at as low as 20%, others with 60%. You must set your own goal, calculate your selling prices based on cost, consider the other factors mentioned

above, and then establish your final menu prices.

Remember, also, that the cost percent of an individual menu item is not always critical. Consider the following calculation concerning two alternative menu items and their gross profit. Gross profit is the selling price less the cost of sales, or food cost.

Item	Cost price	Selling price	Cost %	Gross profit
1	$4.00	$8.00	50.0	$4.00
2	1.00	4.00	25.0	3.00

In this illustration, all other things being equal, you would be better off to sell item 1 rather than item 2. Item 1 has a higher food cost percent, but it also has a higher gross profit. For each of item 1 you sell with a 50% food cost you will have a $4 gross profit, versus only $3 with item 2 even though it only has a 25% food cost.

There is a saying in the restaurant business that you put your net profit (that stems from gross profit) in the bank, and not your cost percentages. Use cost percentages as a starting point for calculating your prices, but don't ignore the gross profit that results.

d. EVALUATE YOUR RESULTS

The last step in this system of food cost control is evaluating the results. Use a form such as that illustrated in Sample #14 to record each individual menu item's cost and selling prices.

You could use this form on a daily or a weekly basis. However, it does require you to take periodic inventories. If you only take inventory once a month, then you will have to limit its use to monthly.

The figures in the "Quantity Sold" column of Sample #14 are your actual quantities of that item sold counted up

SAMPLE #13
RECIPE FORM

Recipe for <u>Veal casserole</u>
Portion size <u>200 grams</u>
Quantity produced <u>50 portions</u>

Ingredient	Quantity	Date: Feb. 15		Date:		Date:	
		Cost	Total	Cost	Total	Cost	Total
Veal stew	10 kg	$3.10	$31.00				
Flour	1 kg	0.50	0.50				
Tomato paste	100 g	$2/kg	0.20				
Chicken stock	4 l	0.50	2.00				
Onions	3 kg	0.75	2.25				
Celery	1.5 kg	0.60	0.90				
Peas	2 kg	0.50	1.00				
Seasonings			0.50				
Total cost			$38.35				
Cost per portion $38.35 ÷ 50			$ 0.77				

Cooking procedure:
1. Brown meat, add flour and tomato paste and mix well.
2. Add chicken stock and simmer for 1 hour.
3. Dice onions and celery and add them, with the peas, cooking until tender.
4. Add seasonings.
5. Serve in 8-oz. casserole dish.

from your sales checks, or tallied up automatically for you in your sales register.

The "Total Standard Cost" column is a multiplication of the "Menu Item Cost" column and the "Quantity Sold" column.

The "Total Standard Revenue" column is a multiplication of the "Menu Item Selling Price" and the "Quantity Sold" column.

The overall "Standard Cost Percentage" can be calculated using information from the "Total Standard Cost" and "Total Standard Revenue" columns as shown in Sample #14.

Finally, on this form, you must calculate and record your "Actual Cost Percentage" for that period. Your accounting records and an actual physical inventory must provide this information. The actual food cost figure is calculated as follows:

Beginning of the period inventory +
Food purchases for the period -
End of the period inventory =
Actual food cost

Note that in the "Actual Cost Percentage" calculation, the denominator is the same as in the "Standard Cost Percentage" calculation. The two amounts should be the same unless errors have occurred, such as in making change.

The difference between the standard food cost and actual food cost percentages can then be calculated. You must expect some difference (usually 0.5% above or below would be normal). For example, if your standard food cost for this period is 38.7%, as shown in Sample #14, then you could expect the actual to be somewhere between 38.2% and 39.2%.

The reason for this is that your standard recipe costs are based on everything going as planned. This type of perfection doesn't usually happen because food can spoil, recipes may not be followed exactly, and other deviations can occur.

Note that, when you calculate your standard cost percent for the following period (see Sample #15), it will change from the current period. You might well ask how this is possible since you are using standard, or set, costs. The answer is that there will likely be a change in the sales mix during the following period. The sales mix refers to what customers decide to eat from your menu offerings from period to period.

Increases and decreases in consumption of each menu item will occur. In our example, 2,000 of item 1 were sold in period 1, and only 1,720 were sold in period 2. Similar changes occurred in other menu items. This is normal, and since your menu item cost and selling prices in Sample #14 for period 1 are based on a certain actual sales mix, when that sales mix changes in subsequent periods, so will your standard cost percent result. However, your actual cost percent will also change, so you are still able to compare oranges with oranges, and your only concern is that the difference between the two figures is within an acceptable limit.

In Sample #15 for period 2 there are changes from period 1. The standard food cost has changed from period 1, where it was 38.7%, to 39.5% in period 2. The actual cost percent has also changed from 38.8% to 40.4%. However, in period 2 the difference is 0.9%, which is a bit outside the suggested allowable difference of 0.5%. In your restaurant, you might want to question why there is this much difference. Once you find the cause, you can then tighten up controls to help ensure the same problems do not occur again.

e. LIQUOR

If you plan to serve alcoholic beverages in your restaurant, you must establish a system for liquor control. Because alcoholic beverages are very apt to "evaporate" or be removed if left unattended, it is extremely important that the person responsible for

SAMPLE #14
STANDARD VERSUS ACTUAL COST FORM
PERIOD 1

Period 1					
Menu item	Menu item		Quantity sold	Total standard cost	Total standard revenue
	Cost	Selling price			
1	$2.10	$6.00	2,000	$4,200.00	$12,000.00
2	1.25	2.75	1,800	2,250.00	4,950.00
3	1.50	5.50	940	1,410.00	5,170.00
4	0.75	2.00	600	450.00	1,200.00
5	4.00	6.50	490	1,960	3,185.00
TOTALS				$10,270.00	$26,505.00

$$\text{Standard cost percent} = \frac{\text{Total standard cost}}{\text{Total standard revenue}} = \frac{\$10,270}{\$26,505} \times 100 = 38.7\%$$

$$\text{Actual cost percent} = \frac{\text{Total actual cost}}{\text{Total actual revenue}} = \frac{\$10,284}{\$26,505} \times 100 = 38.8\%$$

$$\text{Difference} = 0.1\%$$

receiving and storing them be there at the time of delivery.

Wherever possible you should do the receiving yourself. If this is not practical, delegate this important task to a responsible, honest individual. It is also preferable that the receiver is not the same person who does the ordering.

You may have to advise suppliers to deliver only between limited hours when the receiver is available for that particular task. You should also ask that suppliers provide invoices with each shipment of items. Without an invoice, it is difficult for the person responsible for receiving to check all details.

1. Basic storeroom requirements

Liquor inventory in your storeroom at any one time can amount to several thousand dollars. Liquor is money; therefore, it should be treated as money is and with a great deal more security than is often the case in the typical beverage operation.

This security begins with good storeroom design. The storeroom should

Period 2					
Menu item	Menu item		Quantity sold	Total standard cost	Toal standard revenue
	Cost	Selling price			
1	$2.10	$6.00	1,720	$3,612.00	$10,320.00
2	1.25	2.75	1,830	2,288.00	5,033.00
3	1.50	5.50	760	1,140.00	4,180.00
4	0.75	2.00	740	555.00	1,480.00
5	4.00	6.50	500	2,000.00	3,250.00
TOTALS				$9,595.00	$24,263.00

Standard cost percent = $\dfrac{\text{Total standard cost}}{\text{Total standard revenue}}$ = $\dfrac{\$9,595}{\$24,263}$ x 100 = 39.5%

Actual cost percent = $\dfrac{\text{Total actual cost}}{\text{Total actual revenue}}$ = $\dfrac{\$9,802}{\$24,263}$ x 100 = 40.4%

Difference = 0.9%

be difficult, if not impossible, to enter even by professional thieves. You may even need to consider electronic alarm systems to help prevent unauthorized entry.

Your storeroom should have no windows. If it has, you must consider bricking them up or using steel bars across them if your local fire code allows it.

To prevent other types of loss (for example, evaporation or deterioration loss for wines), the storeroom needs to be adequately ventilated and the temperature properly controlled.

2. Perpetual inventory cards and requisitions

Perpetual inventory cards are recommended for all items carried in the beverage storeroom. In addition, requisitions should be used to allow authorized employees to receive items from the beverage storeroom. Perpetual inventory cards and requisitions for storeroom control were discussed in chapter 15.

3. Par stock

As an aid to knowing the quantity of each item to requisition each day, the bar should be provided with a par stock list. This list will name the person responsible for requisitioning the quantity of items required to bring the quantity on hand up to the par, or required, level.

You will have to change these par stock lists when necessary (for example, with a change of season, or when customers' drinking habits change or when you notice bartenders are continually running out of a particular brand during a shift).

Even with a par stock list, it is not always possible for a bar to replenish its stock each day exactly to the par stock level since there may be partly empty bottles in the bar. Therefore, a system of full bottle requisitioning for each empty bottle turned in by the bartender is often used.

Empty bottles are returned to the storeroom with the requisitions and are matched up, bottle for bottle, with full ones. The empty bottles should then be collected for recycling, returned to the supplier (if there is a refundable deposit), or destroyed in accordance with local or other laws where applicable.

4. Bottle coding

Some establishments issue full bottles only after they have been coded with a difficult to duplicate coding device. In such cases, empty bottles returned for replacement with full ones should be checked to ensure they have this code on them.

This control does not prevent a dishonest bartender from bringing in privately purchased bottles, selling the contents, not recording the sales, and pocketing the cash. However, it does reduce that likelihood, since spot control checks by you will show whether or not all bottles at the bar are properly coded. Even with that spot check, you must still be alert to a bartender transferring the contents of a privately purchased bottle to an empty, coded one before selling the contents and keeping the cash.

After empty bottles have been exchanged each day for full ones, the stock at the bar should be at par, adjusted, where necessary, for partly full bottles. This par stock should be checked from time to time immediately after it has been replenished to ensure that par stock levels are correct.

5. Theft or fraud

With the methods outlined above, you should have good control over your storeroom. Control of the bar area itself is more difficult. This is the area where most liquor losses occur.

There are many opportunities for theft or fraud if a bartender or beverage server is dishonest. Some practices to watch out for are:

(a) Underpouring drinks by, let us say, one-sixth the normal measure, not recording the sale of each sixth drink, and pocketing the cash from that drink.

(b) Using personal drink measuring devices (shot glasses or jiggers) that are smaller than the house ones, with the objective of achieving item (a) above.

(c) Diluting liquor with water and keeping the cash from the additional drinks sold.

(d) Bringing in liquor purchased personally, selling the contents, not recording the sales, and pocketing the cash.

(e) Not recording the sales of individual drinks until they add up to the normal number of drinks from a full bottle, and recording the sale as a full-bottle sale. Since the full-bottle sale price would generally be less than the accumulated sales of individual drinks, the bartender can then pocket the difference.

(f) Substituting a house brand for a premium brand (that usually sells at a higher price), charging for the premium brand, and pocketing the difference.

(g) Selling drinks, recording them as spilled, complimentary, or a walk-out, and pocketing the cash.

(h) Overcharging the number of drinks served to a group of customers who are running up a tab to be paid later.

(i) If automatic drink measuring and dispensing devices are used, obtaining the contents for, let us say, five drinks and spreading this content into six glasses, and pocketing the cash from the sixth drink.

(j) Overpouring drinks (and under-pouring others to compensate) to encourage a guest to leave a large tip or "buy" the bartender a drink.

(k) Using private sales checks rather than the ones authorized by the establishment.

(l) Reusing an already paid sales check.

These are only some of the many common dishonest practices that take place. Management awareness and supervision can be a preventive measure. In particular, look for collections of toothpicks, matches, small coins, or any similar item that a bartender may have at the working station to keep track of how much to remove in cash at the end of the shift.

If necessary, you may have to hire one of the many security firms who use trained "spotters." They are experts at posing as regular bar customers and observing common forms of bartender theft.

If you do employ such people, tell them in advance what your policies, systems, rules, and prices are so they know what to look for.

6. Standard cost control

To have complete liquor cost control, you must have standard recipes for each type of drink. It may seem strange to talk about recipes for liquor control, but even defin-

ing the amount of liquor to be served in a standard measure constitutes a recipe.

Since most drinks are simply a standard portion of liquor, usually measured by some type of pouring or measuring device, the recipes are generally easy to prepare. This standard measure should include the amount of ice, water, or soft drink or mineral water to include.

For cocktails, the recipes will be more lengthy, since they must include the quantities of all liquor ingredients used and, where required, the garnish (such as cherry, olive, or fruit slice) to be included. These food ingredients are usually considered part of the beverage cost and must be part of the recipe.

The type and quantity of ice in cocktails, and the mixing method used, are quite important (and therefore should be included in the recipe) since they affect the quantity and quality of the drink.

Once all recipes are developed, they should be written down with a copy for each bartender. It is important that all bartenders are familiar with and abide by each recipe, since consistent quantity and quality of drink served will lead to customer satisfaction.

After you have the recipes, you can then calculate the standard cost of each drink offered. Only by calculating this cost can you establish selling prices that will give you an appropriate beverage cost percent. You can use Sample #13 as a form for calculating beverage standard costs.

The standard cost of each drink is what the cost should be if all procedures are correctly followed. These standard drink costs should be updated when ingredient purchase costs change.

It serves no purpose to prepare standard recipes showing beverage quantities to be served for each separate type of drink unless you provide your bartenders with appropriate measuring devices such as shot glasses and jiggers. Allowing bartenders to free pour liquor is asking for trouble even if bartenders complain that measuring slows them down.

Your bartenders' measuring devices must be checked from time to time to ensure that devices that contain a smaller measure have not been substituted.

Once you have completed these preliminary steps, you can then use the same type of standard cost control illustrated earlier for food. Use Samples #14 and #15 for calculating your standard and actual liquor cost percentages.

f. LABOR COST

Labor cost is another high component of total restaurant operating costs. Before you open your restaurant, you need to carefully plan your staffing requirements and calculate what your total labor cost is going to be. This tentative figure will provide you with a standard labor cost against which you can compare your actual cost when you are in business.

The following figures show one way to calculate a standard labor cost. They are for illustrative purposes only and are not necessarily typical of what your labor cost might be. The figures are for a 50-seat coffee shop open from lunchtime until 8:00 p.m., where the owner acts as host/cashier.

1 cook x 8 hours x $7.50 =	$ 60.00
1 sandwich/salad maker x 8 hours x $5.00 =	40.00
1 pot/dishwasher x 8 hours x $4.50 =	36.00
3½ servers x 8 hours x $5.00 =	140.00
1½ buspersons x 8 hours x $4.00 =	48.00
Total daily cost	$324.00

If the anticipated average daily sales were $1,000, the labor cost percent would be:

$$\frac{\$324}{\$1,000} \times 100 = 32.4\%$$

This cost percent is not untypical for the restaurant industry. However, note that this figure excludes any fringe benefits that are required by law to be paid to employees. The figure also excludes any salary paid to the owner.

You might want to use the chart at the bottom of this page as a guide to staffing for various types of foodservice operation.

With references to these figures, note that your restaurant's menu, style of service, season of year, and other factors dictate the number of staff you need. The figures should be used only as a rough guide and be adapted to your conditions.

g. INDUSTRY STANDARDS

Standard industry percentages for food, beverage, and labor costs are frequently

---

Staffing Guidelines

	Coffee shop	Family dining room	Gourmet restaurant
Servers	1 per 25 seats	1 per 20 seats	1 per 15 seats
Buspersons	1 per 5 servers	1 per 4 servers	1 per 2 servers
Cooks	1 per 120 meals	1 per 100 meals	1 per 80 meals
Dishwashers	1 per 150 meals	1 per 100 meals	1 per 100 meals
Host(ess)	1 per 10 servers	1 per 8 servers	1 per 4 servers

published in trade magazines. Alternatively, they may also be available for various types of restaurant in your area from the local restaurant association branch.

h. COMPUTERIZED CONTROLS

The control systems outlined in this chapter for food, beverage, and labor use manual methods. However, many computerized systems are available today. Some systems use programs that can operate on a personal computer, and some work in conjunction with a sales register. To find out about these systems, talk to computer or restaurant sales register companies to see what they have available that might be appropriate for your operation.

Also, if you would like to learn more about food, beverage, and labor cost controls (including computer applications) the following books will be useful:

(a) *Principles of Food, Beverage, and Labor Cost Controls* by Paul R. Dittmer and Gerald G. Griffin. (New York: Van Nostrand Reinhold, 1984).

(b) *Food and Beverage Control* by Douglas C. Keister. (Englewood Cliffs, N.J.: Prentice-Hall, 1977).

(c) *Food and Beverage Operation: Cost Control and Systems Management* by Charles Levinson. (Englewood Cliffs, N.J.: Prentice-Hall, 1989).

17
PERSONNEL

As a restaurateur, you will have some legal requirements concerning your employees. Some of these requirements include minimum wage levels, the provision of statutory holidays, fair employment practices, the right of employees to collective bargaining and unions, provision of safety standards, and regulatory pay withholdings such as income tax and unemployment insurance. You must be familiar with current government requirements in these and similar matters. In addition, you need to have some sort of employee practices, or personnel policies.

a. JOB DESCRIPTIONS

One of the first steps is to develop job descriptions for each type of job or employee position in your restaurant. In a very small restaurant, the job description may be as simple as deciding that an employee needed as a server must welcome customers pleasantly and look after their needs. A prospective employee being interviewed for this job is simply told what the job entails.

1. Written descriptions

In larger restaurants, each job is more complex and it may be difficult, particularly if there are several different jobs that need to be filled, to remember the many functions that each separate job entails. For that reason, it is preferable to put job descriptions into writing. Then, when an employee is to be hired, a copy of the job description will be immediately available.

No standard job descriptions fit every restaurant. Although there will be some common elements in job descriptions for any particular job type, such as a server or cook, the description for each individual restaurant must be written for that restaurant.

Job descriptions must be kept simple, must be easily understood, and should include the skills, if any, required to perform well in the job. For example, a job description for a position that requires the employee to deal with the public should include the fact that an ability to get along with the public is a skill requirement.

2. Job duties

In addition, for each job description there should be a matching set of job responsibilities that shows in detail the entire range of responsibilities for that job. In this way, both you and the employees are sure what the job responsibilities are, and not what each of you thinks they are.

A list of job duties should not be too detailed, but it should contain sufficient information to cover the main job duties and when those duties are to be carried out.

b. EMPLOYEE SELECTION

Once job skills have been defined through job descriptions and job duty lists, the next step is to match the appropriate employees with the positions you have available.

1. Appropriate pay

Before hiring employees, establish appropriate levels of pay for each specific job. Survey similar types of restaurants in the area to determine the rates they pay and then set a competitive hourly rate or monthly salary.

2. Finding applicants

Advertising for employees can be done informally through family connections or friends. This is certainly a cost free method. Some restaurants advertise positions in local newspapers to encourage as many prospective applicants as possible to apply, although this does cost money.

Some restaurants have found it useful to offer current employees an incentive in the form of a cash or other reward if they bring in a successful applicant who stays with the operation for a minimum period of time (such as six months).

Community colleges or other schools that offer restaurant courses may be another source of applicants. Colleges and universities may also make job opening bulletin boards available to you so that you can post open positions that you have.

You might also want to consider employing people with disabilities. Training may take a little longer, but they will reward you with their loyalty and you may be able to obtain wage subsidies for employing them.

Sometimes it is useful to use personnel agencies (whose offices are generally found only in the larger cities) to seek out needed employees. If the personnel agency is provided with job descriptions of positions that you need to fill, their employees are skilled at matching potential candidates. This can be an expensive method of hiring, but it does offer a prescreening service.

Prescreening can be a time-consuming task of sifting through applications and then interviewing. The time saved by using a personnel agency may be worth the cost.

3. Application form

If you plan to hire employees yourself, an application form should be used each time a person applies for a job. Even if a position is not open when someone asks about a job vacancy, it is a good idea to have the person complete an application form anyway. A few days or weeks from now, because of staff turnover, a vacancy for someone with just those qualifications may arise.

Application forms are useful for summarizing, in an orderly fashion, basic information about job applicants. The forms permit initial screening without having to interview each applicant. A typical application form is illustrated in Sample #16. This form can be modified to suit the particular needs of your restaurant.

c. INTERVIEWING

Interviewing all candidates who have been prescreened through an application form can take a considerable time. If you have five or six prospective applicants for a job, you might spend up to an hour with each one. This is going to use up a large part of a working day. You need to take time in interviewing to ensure the person you hire has the best combination of both technical and human skills to fit into your restaurant.

Conduct all interviews in some private area or office. Have the prospective employee's application form in front of you. You should be familiar with it so you can ask questions about previous education or experience. A prepared list of questions to ask all applicants is useful, since consistency of evaluation is important.

You should ask questions about the employee's present job (assuming he or she has one) and why he or she wishes to leave that job. You might want to find out what the applicant's career expectations are; in other words, is the applicant too ambitious for the kind of job you can offer and the wage or salary you can afford? If technical skills in specific areas are required (for example, specialized cooking), ask enough questions so that you know the applicant has the necessary competence in those areas.

SAMPLE #16
EMPLOYMENT APPLICATION FORM

EMPLOYMENT APPLICATION

Position applied for:_____   Date:_____

How did you hear about this possible job opening?_____

_____

Are there any reasons you may be unable to carry out some of the normal job duties in this

position?_____

If yes, explain_____

Name: _____

Address:_____

City:_____ Postal Code:_____ Tel:_____

What experience, training, or education have you had that would qualify you for this job?

_____

_____

Why are you interested in this job?_____

Are you available for work:

Saturdays_____   Evenings 4-12_____

Days 8-4_____   Sundays_____

Are you now employed?_____   If so, where?_____

References:

1. _____

2. _____

3. _____

Please sign below if you will consent to present or prior employers' release of information or discussion of previous performance with us.

Signature of applicant_____

1. Opportunity for questions

The prospective employee should have an opportunity to ask questions. You should provide a job description, and be specific about working hours, rates of pay, days off, and all other matters regarding your restaurant's working conditions.

If an employee being hired is to report to a supervisor, rather than to you, have the prospective employee and the supervisor meet. Let the supervisor have input into the final selection of the candidate. If the supervisor is to do a good job, there must be compatibility between that supervisor and any employee hired.

2. Make notes

During the interview, it is useful to make mental or written notes about the candidates and your own reactions. Written notes can be placed directly on the application form. Alternatively, you might choose to use an interview evaluation form such as that illustrated in Sample #17.

If an interview is well prepared and well handled, it can be an excellent screening device. It can reinforce the information on the application form or indicate things that do not show on the application form. Sometimes a second interview is useful to give a clearer reading of your impressions and knowledge about an applicant.

3. References

If references are provided on the application form then, with the applicant's permission, follow up with telephone calls to them. If you do not intend to call them, there is no purpose in asking for them on the application form in the first place.

Note that if an applicant gives his or her present employer as a reference, you should telephone that employer only with the permission of the applicant.

It is generally preferable to talk directly to previous employers and supervisors, and to any other individuals identified for reference purposes. Telephone reference comments are easy for you to record, and those giving information on the telephone are more likely to be candid than if they were required to provide the reference in the form of a letter.

Some questions that can be asked of previous employers include: applicant's job title, tasks performed, dates of employment, reason for leaving, quality of work, absenteeism and punctuality, personal characteristics, strengths, weaknesses, overall effectiveness, would you rehire, if not, why not?

With the information from the employment application, the interview, and the reference checks, you are now in a position to decide which applicant to choose.

4. Probationary period

It is a good idea to hire new employees on a probation basis. The importance of the job or the skill level at which the person was hired will determine the length of the probationary period.

Finally, once you have made the selection, keep the application forms of the candidates not selected. After all, a week or month from now you might find a position opening up in your restaurant that one of the unsuccessful candidates could fill.

d. EMPLOYEE ORIENTATION

Every person you employ should be given an orientation. Many employees are uncomfortable in a new job, and the orientation program serves as an introduction to the new job and your restaurant.

This orientation should be given by you or by the supervisor with whom the employee is to work. The orientation should include not only such basic matters as hours of work and pay days but information about any or all of the following:

(a) Restaurant objectives

(b) A copy of the organization chart (if the restaurant is large enough to need one)

SAMPLE #17
INTERVIEW ASSESSMENT FORM

	ASSESSMENT				
	Excellent	Good	Average	Below average	Poor
1. General appearance and neatness					
2. Conduct during interview (poise, manners, pleasantness, politeness, tact)					
3. Communication skills (use of language, ability to explain)					
4. Apparent desire and initiative					
5. Apparent competence for job (education, previous experience)					

References contacted and comments:

1. _____

2. _____

3. _____

Interviewer's comments and recommendation:

_____

_____

_____

_____

_____

_____

_____

(c) A copy of the job description and job duties

(d) When shifts are changed (frequency) and how much advance notice of change is given if the restaurant has different shifts

(e) Vacation entitlement and other fringe benefits

(f) Dress requirements and/or uniforms if required

(g) Care and responsibility for laundering uniforms

(h) Right to a free meal (or not) during shift

(i) Coffee and/or meal break arrangements

(j) Conduct expected when on duty

(k) Evaluation process

(l) Promotion procedures

(m) Termination procedures

(n) Any special restaurant rules (such as when employees may eat)

(o) Introduction to fellow employees

(p) If warranted, a tour of the restaurant facilities

(q) An opportunity for the employee to ask questions during the orientation

The suggestions on this list can be modified to suit your operation. You should prepare a list appropriate to your own restaurant, deleting or adding items from the above where necessary.

A certain amount of on-the-job training will also probably be necessary. Even if an employee is hired in a position for which he or she has previous experience, each restaurant does have different routines and procedures. These different routines and procedures need to be demonstrated or taught to new employees.

In addition, new employees need to be shown the location of storage areas and supplies, switches, keys, and other items related to the job to be performed. Finally, safety and emergency procedures need to be explained or demonstrated.

e. EMPLOYEE TRAINING

All employees need to be directed. This starts with job descriptions and job orientation, and continues with proper training — that is, demonstrating how you expect employees in various positions to handle themselves on the job. In addition, employees need to know how they are doing on the job. This can be done through periodic employee evaluation (see section f.).

The orientation is just the beginning of the ongoing employee training process. The process includes such matters as telling employees what the restaurant's standards are, how these standards can be met, and what level of performance is expected of them. It also includes teaching them the correct performance procedures and how to adapt to day-to-day situations as they arise.

It should not be the employee's responsibility (even though that is often the case in practice) to train themselves in all these matters. The employee needs to be taught through discussion and demonstration, followed by practice.

In small restaurants, this is usually done on the job by the manager or supervisor. Proper training can reduce employee absenteeism, lower employee turnover, and limit costs due to careless use of supplies and equipment. In addition, it can increase employee morale, cooperation, interest in the job, job knowledge, and productivity, all of which are going to lead to a more satisfied restaurant customer.

How you give this direction depends on your management style (your personality and how you treat people). As the owner/manager of the restaurant, you have a big impact on the work environment and on the motivation of your employees. Take time to assess your management style to ensure that you will help, not hinder, the success of your restaurant by the way you relate to your employees. For further information about management styles, read *Be An Even Better Manager*, another title in the Self-Counsel Series.

1. Task procedures

An important aspect of employee training is to develop task procedures. A task procedure is a series of steps that employees must perform to accomplish a job.

Task procedures can be demonstrated to employees. However, if an employee has to carry out a variety of tasks, it works best if the procedures are detailed step by step in writing.

Written procedures help new employees feel more comfortable — particularly if they are being shown a number of different sets of procedures that their job entails.

For example, for food production employees, your standard recipes (see chapter 16) can incorporate the procedures to follow (to ensure a consistent quality of product) and the portion size to be used (to control food cost).

For a dining room hostess you might need separate sets of procedures for greeting customers, seating customers, handling cash, handling credit cards, and leaving a good final impression.

For food and alcoholic beverage servers you might need separate sets of procedures for greeting customers, taking food orders, taking beverage orders, placing food orders, placing beverage orders, serving food, serving beverages, checking back during the meal, presenting sales checks, handling cash payments, and handling credit payments.

As an example, the following might be a set of procedures that you require an employee to follow when opening and serving a bottle of wine:

(a) Place wine glasses at the point of the table setting's knife.

(b) Serve wine before the food it is to accompany, or with the food, but never afterwards.

(c) Serve wine from the right of the guest if possible, with the wine bottle held in your right hand.

(d) Do not lift glasses from the table to fill them with wine.

(e) When pouring, grasp the wine bottle around its middle, and not by the neck or by the base, since the middle is where the point of balance is. If a bottle is held by its neck or base it is much more difficult to hold steady. To help hold the bottle steady while pouring, the index finger can be pointed forward to the neck of the bottle.

(f) Do not pour wine from too great a height, or with the neck of the bottle resting on the rim of the glass. Pour from a height of about 2 to 3 inches.

(g) Do not fill glasses to the brim. If the wine glass is a small one, fill it two-thirds full. If it is a large one, then half full is appropriate. The reason is that the taster should have enough room in the glass to swirl the wine to speed the release of its bouquet.

(h) As each glass is filled, give the bottle a slight twist to the right as it is raised. This helps ensure that any remaining drops of wine on the bottle's lip will not fall on the table but will run around the lip and then back inside the bottle's neck as the bottle is brought upright.

2. Communication

Another aspect of training is communication. Establishing written job descriptions, producing an orientation manual, preparing and demonstrating task procedures are all methods of communicating. So is management or supervisory observation to ensure that employees are performing as desired, correcting them by further reinforcement demonstrations when they are not, and praising them when they are.

Fostering teamwork is also a method of communication and motivation. Teamwork must prevail between food preparation employees and serving employees. Teamwork must also exist between hosting employees, serving employees, and bus personnel. Teamwork is necessary to achieve the goal of having satisfied customers. For example, even though food production employees have no direct contact with guests, they must be made to understand that promptly prepared food is necessary for customer satisfaction, that customer satisfaction can lead to higher tips, and that food production employees will share in these higher tips (because in most restaurants a percentage of all tips is usually given to kitchen employees).

Another aspect of management communication is to solve problems when there is disharmony between employees. Problems can be solved by taking the following steps:

(a) Determine the cause of the problem

(b) Consider alternative solutions to the problem

(c) Discuss these alternatives with the employees involved

(d) Implement the most appropriate solution

(e) Observe whether the implemented solution is working, and if it is not, try some other alternative

3. Importance of service and product knowledge

Although training of all employees in your operation is important, nowhere is it more important than with those employees who deal directly with your customers — that is, your hosting and serving personnel. To the customer, these employees represent your operation, make the first impression customers will have of it, and create the ongoing goodwill that is a necessary part of any successful restaurant operation.

In addition to knowing the procedures for each of their tasks, serving staff must also be knowledgeable about each of the food and alcoholic beverage products on your menus and drink lists. If they are not familiar with each product, they cannot provide customers with the information customers need to make decisions.

To help in this regard, you should produce a descriptive list of each product you offer. For alcoholic beverages this would generally only need to include the ingredients used. For food items, however, it should include the ingredients (including special spices), preparation method, how the item is served including its garnish, and, in some cases, how long the preparation time is.

With food items it is also a good idea to have serving employees taste each dish since this reinforces in their minds what is in the item and how it is prepared.

In all cases, serving employees must know the prices of items without having to refer to menus or drink lists.

4. Methods of motivating employees

There are several techniques you can use to help motivate your employees. One of these is to have periodic staff meetings at which you can discuss with employees how the restaurant is doing. In a small operation you may be able to meet with all employees on a monthly basis. In a large operation you may have to limit participation to one or two representatives from each department.

The purpose of these meetings is not to reveal confidential financial information about your restaurant, but rather to solicit comments and ideas from employees about what you can do to help them do a more effective job and what kind of ideas they may have to make your operation more efficient. The objective is to involve your employees more directly in how the restaurant is managed.

At some of these meetings, you might also want to invite special outside guests who can talk about improved selling techniques or special problems (such as how to spot forged currency or travelers checks).

Another method of motivating employees might be to encourage them to take restaurant industry educational courses. You can also offer to pay part or all of the cost of each course upon successful completion.

Another idea might be to offer an incentive for high performance levels. For example, you might have a periodic award for the server who generates the most dollar sales per guest served or most sales from wine with meals. In fact, to involve more employees, you could have first, second, and third place prizes. The rewards do not have to be expensive. They could take the form of a free meal for the employee and a spouse or companion at your restaurant, or you might be able to barter with a nearby theater by offering that business's management, for example, two free meals at your restaurant for two free tickets to their theater.

The increased sales generated by motivated employees should more than cover the cost of the incentive. A further incentive to serving employees is that as they increase sales, their tips will also increase.

Competitive incentive rewards should not be conducted over too long a time. Even a monthly incentive may be too long to maintain employee enthusiasm. Weekly incentives are probably best.

Further, you should change the incentive from time to time to provide variety and ensure that employees who are the best at achieving one type of incentive do not win all the time.

5. Employee morale

Closely linked to employee motivation is employee morale, and this is a key ingredient in retaining employees. If morale is good, employees will normally be more productive. Good working conditions also help in maintaining good morale.

Remember, each time a valuable employee leaves and has to be replaced, it can cost several hundred dollars to recruit and train a replacement employee, thus adding considerably to your labor cost — which for many restaurants can account for 40¢ of each sales dollar.

6. Quality of service

The result of your employee training endeavors can often be measured in the quality of service you provide your customers.

Quality of service is a matter that customers react to in either a positive or negative way based on each individual's expectations. Service is an intangible part of your business, but objectives for certain aspects of service can be formulated and stated in terms of time. For example, what is the maximum time that you will have a customer wait before he or she is —

(a) seated when there is space available?

(b) seated at the table before a menu is presented?

(c) asked by a server to order from the menu?

(d) served with alcoholic beverages after placing an order?

(e) served with food after placing an order?

(f) presented with the sales check after it is requested?

(g) provided with change when payment is made in cash? and

(h) provided with a completed credit card voucher when payment is made by credit card?

It is not good enough, however, to unilaterally formulate these objectives. They should be established by learning first what level of service your customers expect. This can be done by asking a sample of them what they perceive the time frames should be. This may not be easy to do because it is likely that most customers have not quantified the various situations detailed above in terms of time frames, even though they may know subconsciously that they have or have not received what they feel is good service.

Once your objectives are established with feedback from customers, they must be communicated clearly to employees. You must subsequently use observation to determine if your time objectives are being met. You may then find that adjustments are required either to the time frames or to your staffing levels.

Another way to determine the quality of your restaurant's service level from the customers' perspective is to distribute a questionnaire from time to time. This questionnaire should be short, with only four or five questions about various aspects of your service.

Many restaurants find it a good idea to print these questions on the reverse side of sales checks and have servers when presenting them at the end of a meal as customers to take a few moments to answer the questions.

Obviously you don't want regular customers to complete questionnaires on every visit. Your servers will know who these regular customers are and can tell them not to bother with the questions unless they choose to do so.

One other factor about your service quality that you might want to test concerns telephone reservations. Many businesses lose sales because employees who answer telephones have not been trained to do the job properly. Training should be followed by monitoring. One way to monitor is for you to phone in and pretend to be a customer making a reservation.

f. EMPLOYEE EVALUATION

The final step in personnel planning is employee evaluation. In a very small restaurant, this can simply be management observation. A competent owner can quickly determine if a new employee is fitting in and able to do a good job.

Incompetent employees may have to be released or, if positions are available, moved to a job where the demands are not as great. Competent employees should be encouraged to continue to do a good job and be challenged with more responsibility or promoted when possible.

1. Formal evaluation

In a restaurant with more than a few employees, evaluations may be carried out once or twice a year in a formal way with an evaluation form for each employee. The employee should be allowed to read the evaluation and, indeed, even sign the completed evaluation form to indicate agreement with it. A sample evaluation form is illustrated in Sample #18.

Evaluate employees with reference to the whole job. For example, an employee working with the public should be evaluated on his or her performance with the customers, with other employees, and with the supervisor, not just on one of those three specific relationships.

The evaluation must be carried out objectively, despite the fact that the process itself is a subjective one. In other words, personal bias for or against an employee should not be allowed.

Even if the evaluation is not written down, the results of the evaluation, both the good and the bad points, should be discussed with the employee. Communicating with employees concerning both poor and excellent performance is preferable to not communicating at all.

SAMPLE #18
EMPLOYEE EVALUATION FORM

EMPLOYEE EVALUATION

Employee name_____   Position_____

Date employed_____   Date of evaluation_____

	Excellent	Good	Average	Below average	Poor
KNOWLEDGE OF JOB: Clear understanding of dutires related to job. Is employee well-suited? Able to handle equipment related to job?					
DEPENDABILITY: Conscientious; punctual; reliable with respect to attendance, relieving other employees.					
COURTESY: Is employee courteous to guests, fellow employees, supervisor?					
COOPERATION: Ability and willingness to work with supervisors and subordinates.					
WORK QUALITY: Thoroughness, neatness, completeness, and accuracy of work.					
WORK QUANTITY: Volume of work acceptable under normal conditions and pressures?					
PERSONAL QUALITIES: Personality, sociability, integrity, leadership potential.					
APPEARANCE: Hygiene and neatness, considering the job being performed.					

OVERALL PERFORMANCE: SATISFACTORY ❑   UNSATISFACTORY ❑

Supervisor's signature_____

Employee's signature_____

2. Pay raises

The evaluation process includes consideration of pay raises at least once a year. Regardless of the type of restaurant, the factors that influence the amount of a wage increase (in the absence of a union contract) are the same. They are:

(a) The restaurant's ability to pay higher wages

(b) The demands of the job

(c) The pay rate compared to similar jobs in other restaurants

(d) The results of the employee's evaluation

(e) The general inflation rate

(f) The local supply and demand for employees

3. Promotions

Whenever job vacancies arise, it is usually preferable to see if a replacement can be found from within the restaurant, particularly if this will create a promotion for an employee. Employees who know there are advancement opportunities within the restaurant have an incentive to stay and generally have a higher job performance level.

Although seniority is sometimes made the basis for promotion into a vacant position, that type of promotion should only occur if the person has the qualifications and capabilities to do the job, particularly if the job has a measure of responsibility and authority. This is where the employee evaluation form can be helpful.

4. Discipline

Every restaurant must have employment rules and regulations that employees are to follow. Some of these rules and regulations are restrictive, others are for safety reasons, and yet others are to protect the rights of employees.

Making sure employees know and understand these rules is part of the orientation/training process. In some cases when rules are broken, employees should be reminded of the rules. Often a brief discussion with the employee will be all that is necessary. In other cases, some disciplinary action may be necessary. This action could be in the form of a written memo to the employee concerned.

The memo might mention the incident that occurred, what action will be taken as a result (this could simply be that the memo is being written as a reminder), any further action that might be taken if the rule is broken again, a time that a review of the situation will occur, and provision for the employee to acknowledge receipt of the warning or disciplinary action.

Make a copy of the memo for the employee, one for the employee's supervisor (if there is one), and one (preferably with the employee's signature on it) for your file.

5. Termination

At times employees must be disciplined in the severest way by terminating their employment. This is a last resort since it should only happen in the most critical of situations, and you should show cause for dismissal. Cause can often be justified by the number of disciplinary action memos in an employee's file.

Also, one of the values in having clearly written job descriptions is that they can indicate at the time the employee is hired the level of job performance required. If the employee has failed to meet that level, and this can be supported by memos in the employee's file, then cause can be documented.

If it is necessary to terminate an employee, this should be done in private on a one-to-one basis. The employee should be given the reasons for termination. A good way to round out the termination process is to emphasize the employee's strong points and perhaps suggest alternatives for that person's future.

g. EMPLOYEE RECORDS

Any restaurant must maintain some sort of records about its employees. This record might simply be a file folder containing the application form of each employee on payroll, with a notation on the form of the employee's current wage or salary.

But even a small restaurant has staff turnover, and may hire additional employees on a seasonal basis. In such cases, it is not always easy to mentally store all the facts about present and past employees. Therefore, an employee record card or sheet is recommended for each employee hired. An illustration of such a card is shown in Sample #19.

This card could be hand drawn if the number of employees is few, or be pre-printed if there are many employees. On this card, record information such as the date each employee was hired, the position, and the initial rate of pay. Any subsequent changes in the status of each employee can be recorded beside the date of the change. Changes in status include such items as moving to another job within the restaurant, a change in wage or salary, or the date employment was terminated, with the reason in the "Comment" column. These record cards are useful for providing up-to-date information about current employees and also about former employees who are being re-employed or about whom you have received reference requests from another employer.

How long should the files of past employees be kept? Between two and five years is reasonable. When the files are no longer to be kept, all the information in them should be destroyed. Since employee files contain confidential information, they should be available only to you, to a responsible person who is authorized to keep employee files up to date, and to the employee concerned.

h. FURTHER READING

If you would like to do further reading about personnel practices, the following books are recommended:

(a) *The Waiter and Waitress Training Manual* by Sandra Dahmer and Kurt Kahl. (New York: Van Nostrand Reinhold, 1988).

(b) *Professional Dining Room Management* by Carol King. (New York: Van Nostrand Reinhold, 1988).

(c) *Training Foodservice Employees* by Genevieve LaGreca. (New York: Van Nostrand Reinhold, 1988).

SAMPLE #19
EMPLOYEE RECORD CARD

Employee name_____ Date first employed_____

Initial position_____ Starting wage or salary_____

Date	Change of status to:	Wage/salary	Comment

18
MARKETING

When most people hear the word marketing they think only of advertising. Advertising, however, is only one aspect of marketing. Marketing really embraces everything that you do in your restaurant to attract and retain customers.

All restaurants operate in an ever-changing marketing environment. You must continually analyze and evaluate this environment to stay alert to changes that, if not effectively managed, could harm profitability or even the survival of your operation. You must also be aware of new opportunities that arise.

Detailed analysis is a preliminary step in planning your restaurant's marketing. Your objectives will be to retain business, encourage repeat business, and develop new sources of business, all with the ultimate goal of increasing sales and profits. Several types of analysis are possible. Let us look in particular at the following:

(a) Trading area analysis

(b) Competitor analysis

(c) Product analysis

(d) Opportunity analysis

a. TRADING AREA ANALYSIS

If you have done your research, you will have already defined your trading area (see chapter 9). Now you need to do further analysis. A trading area analysis has two sections: an attraction analysis and a business environment analysis.

1. Attraction analysis

It is not hotels, restaurants, or transportation companies that lure people to a community, but rather attractions. You may be able to obtain a considerable amount of additional business from tourists visiting those attractions.

Conduct an attraction analysis to list and evaluate those that are complementary to your business. Make an inventory of these attractions so that the marketing opportunities they present can be considered. For example, if there is a historic site, a museum, or a sports facility in your trading area, visitors to those locations can add considerably to your customer base.

Consider ways in which you can advertise your restaurant at those locations. For example, can you display posters there that advise people that your restaurant is nearby?

2. Business environment analysis

Your area analysis should also include consideration of the business environment to see what changes are taking place. Business environment changes can occur in two ways. First, there are changes that are taking place in society as a whole. These changes could include economic, demographic, and technological ones which affect business generally.

Second, there are changes that affect only local businesses, such as changes in resident or tourist traffic patterns that result in an increase or decrease in demand for restaurants in your area. You need to be aware of these changes so that you can adapt to them.

b. COMPETITOR ANALYSIS

Competitor analysis requires you to obtain and evaluate information about competitors. This information can be used in developing competitive strategies. Most restaurants are small businesses whose focus is on day-to-day internal operating problems. Because of this, it is probably fair to say that most of them do not have, or do not take, the time to look at the competition.

It is probably also fair to say that, even where operators do consider the competition they do not look at it analytically or consider how they could create a competitive advantage out of it. You can obtain a great deal of competitive information at little or no cost through informal contacts or by observation.

1. Sources of information

Consider the following ways of obtaining information about your competitors:

(a) Visit competitors to monitor their business volumes, find out what their prices are, and review their product quality by eating in their restaurants.

(b) Observe competitor marketing strategies by reviewing their menus and other promotional materials.

(c) Attend local, regional, or national trade association meetings and/or read their newsletters or other publications.

(d) Make personal competitor contacts at association meetings.

(e) Talk with suppliers who trade with competitors.

(f) Hire employees who previously worked for the competition.

(g) Talk with customers who patronize both your restaurant and competitor restaurants.

2. Benefits of competitor analysis

A competitor analysis can give you the following benefits:

(a) Identify the unique selling features of the competition. Unique selling features are the assets that a competitor has that differentiate it from you.

(b) Identify opportunities that competitors have capitalized on that you have not.

(c) Identify opportunities that you have that the competitors do not.

(d) Improve the way in which you view your customers.

(e) Show how customers, given alternatives, make decisions about which restaurant best suits their needs.

(f) Provoke new operating and product ideas that can be introduced to improve your profits.

(g) Aid in forecasting and thus in planning for the future.

(h) Require you to consider what a particular decision will prompt in the way of a response from competitors.

(i) Point to particular aspects of your business that require more attention.

(j) Suggest the need for change in order to maintain a competitive edge.

(k) Indicate competitors' strengths and weaknesses so that strengths can be adapted to and weaknesses exploited.

c. PRODUCT ANALYSIS

Product planning is an essential ingredient of a marketing strategy. Your product is not just the food you serve, but all the factors that customers are exposed to when they visit your premises — the service they receive, the ambience of your restaurant, the cleanliness of your operation, and the friends they might meet when dining in your restaurant.

1. Physical limitations

Even though restaurants have physical limitations (such as the number of customers who can be served at any one time), each restaurant has some flexibility in the way it conceptualizes itself — its atmosphere, image, type of furniture, and decor. It also has flexibility in its management operating style — the level of staffing, quality of service, pricing, and promotion of particular menu items. These product factors can be relatively quickly and easily adjusted to change the product, adapt it to a changing market, or attract a new market.

Even when the physical size of the restaurant or the style of operation is set, your product can be enhanced by adding to it elements that customers will perceive as offering additional value for money. These enhancements might be inducements that appeal to certain segments of the market. For example, you might cooperate with a local sightseeing bus company to include a stop at your restaurant in the price of a tour ticket, or provide an inexpensive toy to children dining at your restaurant with their parents.

2. Location

Another product factor for many restaurants is location. The importance of location to your customers can change over time. If you know how this importance is changing you can adjust other factors to compensate. For example, even though you cannot change the volume of traffic (either pedestrian or automotive) that passes by your restaurant, you can influence the number of people who know that your restaurant is there. For example, added or improved highway signs can influence passing motorists, and sidewalk tent signs can induce passing pedestrians to drop in.

3. Parking

Parking is also a product factor. Is it adequate? If not, is there anything you can do about it? For example, can you cooperate in some way with adjacent premises that have surplus parking space to allow customers of your restaurant to park there?

d. OPPORTUNITY ANALYSIS

Once you are familiar with your area, your competition, and your product, the next step is to identify new market opportunities. These opportunities are the gaps between what customers want and what you and your competition are presently offering. By taking advantage of those opportunities and filling those gaps, you can increase your sales. These opportunities could be internal or external.

1. Internal opportunities

Internal opportunities include such items as —

(a) improving an existing product factor,

(b) introducing a new menu item,

(c) increasing an operating strength,

(d) strengthening an operating weakness, or

(e) raising and improving customer satisfaction.

2. External opportunities

External opportunities exist when you have a chance to increase your market share. Market share increase is concerned with increasing the volume of sales in your present location or with an existing market (type of customer). This increased volume of sales is usually the result of an improved marketing effort.

An external opportunity can also occur when you attempt to increase your sales by expanding into new markets (new types of customers) or locations. For example, this might happen when you open a new restaurant in a second location. Alternatively, it can occur if your restaurant takes over a competitive nearby restaurant.

e. MARKETING PLAN

A marketing plan answers the following five questions:

(a) Where am I now?

(b) Where do I want to be by the end of the next 12 months?

(c) How am I going to get there?

(d) How much am I prepared to spend to get there?

(e) How effective was my plan in getting there?

Your marketing plan begins with stating the objectives you wish to achieve that might help you fill the opportunities or gaps you have identified. Generally, objectives are stated in quantitative terms. For instance, you might decide that you want to increase sales next year by 3% over current year sales or increase average customer spending by $1 in the next six months. As well as stating objectives in quantitative terms, include a time frame so that at the end of that period you can compare what you have achieved with your objectives.

1. Strategies

Once marketing objectives have been established, you must devise one or more strategies that will allow you to achieve those objectives. Here are some examples:

(a) Changing menu prices to influence the sale of the most profitable items. Revised prices could be higher or lower than present ones.

(b) Increasing the satisfaction of present customers by giving them more value for money

(c) Changing the style of service

(d) Improving existing exterior signs to attract more customers

(e) Spending more on advertising to increase customer awareness and attract more customers or to generate more repeat business from present customers

(f) Expanding sales by offering take-out service for certain menu items

Note that in devising strategies you must keep the boundaries of your present trading area in mind. In the short run those boundaries are not likely to change very much, and most of your business, both new and repeat, will be from people living or working within those boundaries or visiting attractions within them. Also, the more distant people are from your location, the less likely it is that they will be repeat customers. Therefore, the largest portion of your marketing budget should be spent on programs that reach people within your trading area.

If you spend money on advertising and promotion to reach people outside those boundaries, you might be wasting money. This does not mean that you cannot go outside your boundaries, but you must carefully evaluate the results.

2. Measuring results

At the end of the period for which you have established objectives, you need to evaluate the results. In other words, you must take each strategy and determine whether or not it contributed to achieving your objectives. Strategies that were not helpful should be dropped, and those that contributed should be used again.

For a detailed discussion of marketing, see *Marketing your Product*, another title in the Self-Counsel Series.

19
ADVERTISING

Regardless of the size of your restaurant, some advertising is necessary and usually worth the cost. Apart from the initial business it brings in, it also has a cumulative effect as customer goodwill is built up and your restaurant gains an identity.

a. PLANNING ADVERTISING

You should view your advertising as an investment rather than an expense. Successful advertising is planned; it doesn't just happen. It should be planned anywhere from six months to one year ahead.

Your reasons for advertising should go beyond simply attracting customers. What will you emphasize in your advertising? Will it be your restaurant name, location, and prices? Or will it be the fact that you are new in business and have something different to offer in your menu? In other words, your advertising should have a purpose.

The question of when you are going to advertise is often answered once your advertising purpose has been determined.

For example, as a new restaurateur, your initial purpose will be to tell potential customers that you are in business. Thus, you want to advertise that fact prior to and for some time after opening.

Later on, your advertising may need to coincide with special events (for example, Mother's Day), or time of the year (for example, the Christmas season) for which you may produce special menus or menu items you can feature.

b. ADVERTISING BUDGETS

Advertising budgets are generally established as a percentage of sales. Some experts say that the percentage should increase when sales decline (since you need the advertising then) and decline when sales increase. Regardless of policy, the objective of advertising is to increase the benefits of advertising within budget limitations.

A typical advertising budget for a restaurant is from 2% to 4% of annual sales. But even among restaurants the percentage can vary. You may have to spend more than your competitors who have been in business for some time. Where competition among established similar restaurants is strong, each of them may have to spend more on advertising, obliging you to do the same.

About 80% of your advertising budget will probably be for newspaper, magazine, radio, television, or similar types of advertising, and the other 20% for developing the advertising message.

If you have enough working capital, you should double your advertising budget during your first year and spend the extra amount within a month or two prior to opening.

For example if your sales goal is $300,000 a year, and your advertising budget is 2% of that, or $6,000 a year, you might well set aside an additional $6,000 of pre-opening working capital for advertising to provide your potential market with information and/or to take away business from your competition.

If your advertising budget is $6,000 a year, that does not mean that you must spend $500 every month. Your budget should be related to the proposed sales each month. For example, if July sales are budgeted for $40,000, your advertising budget for July is $40,000 x 2% = $800, and if budgeted sales for December are $80,000, your advertising budget for that month is $80,000 x 2% = $1,600.

The advertising budget for any particular sales month should not be spent during that month. To benefit from advertising, you must spend the money up to a month ahead. The advertising budget for July's sales should be spent in June, and so on.

Even though there are many advertising vehicles available, you should not use them all, even if you can afford to. Concentrate on one or two. More of one or two is better than less of five or six. Also, within any one medium the same principle applies. For example, it is better to run five advertisements in one newspaper than one advertisement in five.

c. PREPARING YOUR ADVERTISING MESSAGE

The preparation of your advertising message is important. Decide on your objectives, research the media to discover which is likely to be most effective for your purposes (see section d.), and choose your words carefully. You may find that people who work in the media can help you in planning effective advertising campaigns.

You may be able to afford the use of a professional advertising agency. Remember, though, that their commission is usually at least 15% on top of the total cost charged by the newspaper, journal, radio, or other medium used. If you use a direct mail agency, you will also pay a commission, sometimes 20% or more, or else a fixed fee.

Take care in any claims you make about your restaurant and its prices. Untrue, exaggerated, or misleading statements can cause you legal problems. Before your advertisements are finally printed or broadcast, carefully proofread them to weed out any errors. Be particularly careful of advertisements prepared by someone else on your behalf.

d. ADVERTISING MEDIA

Advertising, or sales promotion, can be categorized as either direct or indirect. Direct sales promotion means sending a commercial message to inform the public with the objective of increasing sales.

You can use various forms of advertising media to send an advertising message to potential customers. Whichever medium you eventually select, you must be sure that it is —

(a) within your budget,

(b) compatible with your image and restaurant,

(c) suitable for your market and geographic area of business, and

(d) able to serve your geographic area effectively.

1. Newspapers

Newspapers are a common and popular advertising vehicle for restaurateurs. Newspapers offer flexibility (in size of possible advertisements and the day(s) you wish to advertise) and graphics. If your restaurant only services part of a city, the local community newspaper might be preferable to the large city newspaper. It will also cost less.

Make sure you are familiar with the market area served by the newspaper and obtain its circulation. Newspaper advertising rates are based on circulation — the higher the circulation, the higher the cost. The advertising cost divided by the newspaper's circulation will give you a cost per reader for purposes of comparison.

Newspaper space is sold in lines or inches and columns. For example, a two-column, 25-line advertisement would be charged for at the equivalent of 50 lines.

Newspapers also generally offer special contract rates when you agree to purchase a specified minimum number of column inches over a year. This can significantly reduce your cost per column inch.

Newspapers will often provide advertisement design services as part of the cost of the advertisement.

2. Radio

Local radio stations can often be a useful form of advertising. Radios reach a wide range of customers, although repetitive advertising is generally required for it to have any effect and repetition does cost money.

Radio advertising is usually sold in 10-, 15-, 30-, or 60-second "spots." The 30- and 60-second spots are the most popular. Costs vary depending on time of day, listening audience size, and the particular radio station. Advertising just before the news, and from 7 to 9 a.m., and 4 to 6 p.m., will probably cost more than the same ad halfway through an hour of music.

Find out what the cost per thousand listeners is. For example, if a spot announcement costs $30 and reaches 5,000 people, your cost per thousand listeners is $6. This way you can compare costs from station to station, and from one time period to the next on each station.

Again, as with newspapers, radio stations will often prepare the advertisement and provide this service as part of the advertisement's cost.

3. Television

Television advertising is expensive and is not used often by independent restaurant owners. It does have the advantage of a visual impact that radio does not have but, in addition to the TV station's cost of time, production costs, even for a 30-second ad, can run into tens of thousands of dollars.

4. Magazines

Magazine advertising can be expensive. If your business is localized (as it is for many restaurants), the expense of advertising in this medium may not be worth the cost. An exception might be local magazines, such as tourist visitor guides.

An advantage of magazine advertising is that, unlike radio, television, or newspapers, magazines last for a long time and can be read by a succession of people. However, the small restaurant owner should advertise in them only with caution. Note that magazines need from two to four months lead time to run your advertisement.

5. Direct mail

Direct mail can be an effective form of advertising, particularly if it is selective (for example, mailing the advertising flyer or brochure to customers you have previously served). It is relatively inexpensive and its effectiveness is easy to measure.

Direct mail includes the use of business cards, postcards, coupons, letters, circulars, and even copies of your menus. The rate of return in direct mail campaigns usually averages about 2% or 3%. In other words, if you send out 10,000 circulars, you might expect 200 to 300 people to respond in some way.

6. Directories

Directories, and in particular telephone directory Yellow Pages advertising, are also useful. For example, potential customers may want to phone you to find out your hours or days of opening, or to make reservations.

Since telephone directories are usually published annually, their advertising messages generally have a relatively long life and, apart from any other advertising, are essential for most restaurants.

7. Highway billboards

Billboards can be expensive but are still used by many restaurants where they can be strategically located to catch the eye of potential customers. Billboard advertising is relatively expensive both for billboard rent and advertisement production costs.

8. Your menu

Finally, don't forget that your menu, once customers are in your restaurant, can be an advertising piece.

The way it is typeset and the style of your menu, as well as the ease with which it informs customers, are all advertising factors that can increase your profits. For example, featuring items in bold print is one way to direct attention to items on your menu that yield a high gross profit.

Designing menus is an art, and not one that can be covered in a book of this nature. Observation of other restaurants' menus is one way to learn, and there are some excellent books written on this subject. These books were listed at the end of chapter 3.

Your menu falls into a category of advertising known as sales promotion. Other forms of sales promotion are table top tent cards (advertising daily or weekly menu specials) and displays such as dessert carts.

9. Coupons

You might also consider using coupons. Coupons can take several forms such as offering a stipulated dollar amount off the price of a meal, or offering two meals for the price of one. Some coupons are distributed in newspaper or magazine advertisements, others are sent to potential customers by direct mail, and some are distributed in "entertainment" booklets that are purchased by consumers.

Coupons distributed by direct mail have the advantage of allowing selection of a specific target market and thus generally generate a higher user response. However, printing and postage costs make this a more expensive method of distribution than using a newspaper or magazine advertisement.

Media coupon advertising offers the advantage of flexibility in timing so that the coupon can be coordinated with a newspaper or magazine promotion. The major disadvantage of media coupon distribution is that the coupons may have a low usage or redemption ratio and their effect is probably short-term because customers seeking coupon savings aren't likely to provide long-term repeat business.

Coupon advertising has to be measured on its own merits depending on the facts in each situation. For example, consider the following: a restaurant has completed a coupon campaign offering two meals for the price of one valid during a specific month only. The restaurant's normal average food cost is 40% (meaning that for the coupon meals its food cost will be 80%). There is no additional labor cost to prepare and serve the extra customers the coupons attract since present staff can comfortably handle the additional volume. Any other cost increases (for example, cooking fuel) will be nominal. Some of those attracted by the coupons will drink alcoholic beverages. Normal cost of sales on alcoholic beverages is 30%. The cost of advertising the coupons in local newspapers is $300.

As a result of the campaign, an analysis of sales checks for the two-for-one meals show that food sales were $1,790 and alcoholic beverage sales $496. The restaurant's "profit" on this campaign is:

Additional food sales	$1,790	
Less: food cost 80%	1,432	$358
Additional beverage sales	$ 496	
Less: beverage cost 30%	149	$347
Additional total sales		$705
Less advertising cost		300
Additional "profit"		$405

This is a good profit on an investment of $300 for advertising. However, this additional "profit" of $405 may not be the true profit because some of the customers who used coupons might have patronized the restaurant at regular prices if the coupons had not been available. This can be assessed by seeing if there was a decrease in regular business during that month compared to previous periods.

Also, some of the people who were not previously customers of the restaurant might become regular customers in the future, thus adding to future profits. This can also be assessed by seeing if normal business increases in periods following the coupon campaign.

10. Contra advertising

Contra advertising, also sometimes known as trade-outs or bartering, is based on a product-for-product exchange. For example, a restaurant might make a contra agreement with a radio station. The radio station will run the restaurant's advertisements for "free" and the restaurant will provide radio station representatives with an equivalent amount of "free" meals.

e. INDIRECT SALES PROMOTION

In addition to the direct methods of advertising already detailed, you also have the opportunity of using the following, less direct, forms of advertising.

1. Publicity

Publicity, or public relations, is advertising that you don't have to pay for other than in time. Publicity is both an internal and an external opportunity for increasing sales.

Internal publicity includes how you treat your customers while they are on your premises, and how you treat your employees, since both customers and employees can be goodwill ambassadors for your restaurant.

External publicity means letting people know about the good things your restaurant is doing by releasing "news" items or photographs to local newspapers, radio stations, and even television stations.

For example, if your restaurant sponsors a sports team, or participates in a charitable event, the local news media might like to know about this. Words and pictures go a long way in creating community goodwill that is part of public relations, and this type of advertising can be done with little, if any, cost.

Public relations is what establishes the general view of your restaurant in the eyes of the community. This is not something that can be purchased since it stems from an attitude in the public's mind that has been created by the way you run your restaurant, the way you treat your employees, and the way you handle your customers.

If your public relations are good you will develop goodwill in the community. Poor public relations will likely lead to illwill which can affect your restaurant negatively.

2. Customer relations

Advertising might make customers aware of your restaurant, but it doesn't bring them back the second time. Good service does that. Your service staff must have a thorough knowledge of all your menu items and their prices and be able to develop good customer relations in order to have satisfied customers. This involves such matters as speed in processing guest orders, handling complaints, providing an extra service where possible, and going out of your way in unexpected or emergency situations. Good customer relations will build business through word-of-mouth advertising.

f. RESTAURANT CRITICS

Restaurant critics know less about your business than you do, even when you have only been at it for a week, but you may still have to face their criticisms.

Critics can neither make nor break a good, successful restaurant. Only you can do that. However, critics can help a new, small, unknown restaurant with a good review, or speed up its downfall with a bad review. But don't change your recipes, menus, employees, and operating policies because of what a critic says if the majority of your customers seem satisfied. Some critics write only positive reviews and some can never find anything positive to say about any restaurant. Many of them know little about what they are eating and drinking.

A critic should visit your restaurant anonymously. However, if a critic is known to you, do not offer free food and drink as that may interfere with an objective review. Do, however, encourage a critic to make two or three visits before writing a review.

Finally, if a review of your restaurant is contingent on your advertising in the critic's magazine or newspaper, don't waste your advertising dollars that way.

20
INSURANCE

Before opening, you should map out your insurance program. Every restaurant operates with risk every day. A risk is the possibility of damage, injury, or loss. Generally, a small restaurant is less able to absorb losses from risk, and for this reason it is more important that you understand the kinds of risks that are common and, if necessary, insure yourself against them.

Once the risks are known, policies can be established to minimize them. Almost any type of risk can be insured against, but to insure against every possible risk would be prohibitively costly for most small restaurants.

An important ingredient in insurance coverage is to employ an insurance agent who has had previous experience in handling restaurant coverage. That agent needs to visit your restaurant to view it firsthand and be informed about your operation's insurance requirements. Also, if you are in leased premises, the agent should be given a copy of the lease so he or she can provide any insurance coverage required by the lease contract.

a. BUILDING AND CONTENTS FIRE INSURANCE

If you own your own building, the basic type of insurance coverage required is for loss to building(s) and personal property on a stipulated peril basis (such as fire, lightning, and earthquake).

Generally, building insurance covers all permanent fixtures (including such items as heating, cooling, air-conditioning, elevators, and similar engineering and/or mechanical equipment) as well as signs attached to the restaurant.

Normally one insurance policy is sufficient if you own both the restaurant and contents (equipment, fixtures, and inventory). If the restaurant is leased, the lessor and you (the lessee) should each insure your own assets.

Fire insurance on building and contents is the most frequently purchased insurance. Cost will vary considerably from one situation to another. Most fire insurance policies are written for three-year periods, and commonly the premiums are adjusted annually.

Building and contents insured for fire should be insured at their replacement cost (and not original cost) because that is the amount of money you will need to get back into business in the event of a fire.

Building and contents can be further protected by various types of optional insurance (since a standard insurance policy does not normally include these items) including any or all of the following:

(a) *Extended coverage* covers the property against all direct loss or damage due to such things as explosions, windstorms, hail, riot, aircraft, vehicles, and smoke.

(b) *Glass* insurance protects against replacement of plate glass windows accidentally or maliciously broken.

(c) *Vandalism and malicious mischief* protects against losses caused by either of these possibilities.

(d) *Sprinkler* insurance covers against leakage, freezing, or breakage of sprinkler installations. If this type of insurance is taken out, both building and contents should be insured.

(e) *Flood and earthquake* are optional insurance coverages that should be considered in areas whether either flood or earthquake, or both, are a possibility.

(f) *Sign* insurance covers damage to exterior signs, such as a neon advertising sign, from such things as wind or vandalism.

(g) *Inventory* coverage should also be considered if it is not specifically included in the basic policy. For example, items stored in refrigerators and freezers could spoil in the event of a power outage. However, investigate the cost of this form of coverage. If its cost is greater than any potential loss, then this insurance would not be worthwhile.

(h) *Automobile* insurance may also be necessary. If your restaurant owns one or more vehicles they should be insured. Also, if you require certain employees to use their own vehicles to pick up food or beverages from suppliers you need insurance coverage for this. The reason is that a person injured while an employee was using his or her car on restaurant business might find it more advantageous to sue your restaurant rather than the car's owner.

b. LIABILITY INSURANCE

Your restaurant is liable to claims for alleged injuries to customers, employees, or others with whom you do business. The broadest possible insurance protection that you can buy is a comprehensive general liability policy that covers you against all claims for injuries that occur. This can be supplemented by optional endorsements to cover other specified possibilities.

Optional liability insurance might be required for a restaurant that has a garage or parking lot for the convenience of customers. Two specific types of insurance are necessary: automobile garage liability protects against any liability for bodily injury and property damage caused by an accident in the garage or on the parking lot, and garage keeper's liability covers liability for fire or theft of stored or parked vehicles.

Liability insurance can include not only physical injury, but also damage to the property of others, or even such things as food poisoning lawsuits against a restaurant by customers.

Similarly, if a customer has too much to drink while dining in your restaurant and on leaving is involved in an automobile accident in which someone else is badly or fatally injured, you could be sued because you were responsible for allowing that customer to drink too much while in your restaurant. You can protect yourself against this possibility with the proper liability insurance.

c. CRIME INSURANCE

Your restaurant may frequently have large sums of cash on hand subject to both employee theft and armed robbery.

To protect against such losses, some insurance companies offer blanket crime policies offering complete coverage on a package basis. Although individual types of crime insurance policy are available, blanket insurance is usually cheaper, and since total coverage for the full amount of losses under such policies would be prohibitively expensive, most crime insurance policies include a deductible amount. Some of the crime insurance types of policy are as follows.

Fidelity bonds insure against losses due to theft or other misappropriations of inventory or cash or other business property by employees. Only established losses will be reimbursed.

This policy can be written as a blanket bond to cover all employees or it can be a schedule bond to limit it to those specific positions and employees who handle, or who have access to, cash, inventory, or similar items. In some situations, it may be preferable to bond specific individual employees.

Money and securities insurance covers losses that occur away from the restaurant's premises (for example, a robbery of daily receipts being transported to the bank).

Robbery insurance covers loss of goods stolen where there is an assault or threat of an assault — such as in a hold-up.

Burglary insurance covers the loss of inventory, money, or equipment from a break-in of your premises. Generally there must be signs of a forced entry.

Theft and shoplifting covers loss of inventory, money, or equipment where there is no break-in or burglary involved and items were presumably stolen by employees, customers, or others.

Surety bonds protect you from losses caused by the failure of others to produce on schedule. For example, if you having a new building constructed, and the construction company does not complete the building on time resulting in losses to you, you may recover those insured losses from the insurance company.

d. BUSINESS INTERRUPTION INSURANCE

A standard fire insurance policy pays you only for losses directly due to fire. Other indirect losses, referred to as consequential losses, may be of greater risk to your restaurant than the fire damage itself. They can be protected against by business interruption insurance.

If you have business interruption insurance, the restaurant is reimbursed for loss of earnings, and ongoing expenses that occur (such as interest expense on a mortgage, or rent) until normal business resumes. In addition, payroll costs for key employees can be completely covered, or covered for a specified period of time.

e. WORKERS' COMPENSATION INSURANCE

You must provide your employees with a safe workplace, and safe equipment and tools. Also, you will likely be required, by law, to have workers' compensation insurance. This insurance fund is administered by the jurisdiction in which you operate.

The fund collects premiums from individual businesses. These premiums are generally based on payroll (for example 3% or $3 of insurance per $100 of payroll) according to the particular type of business's accident rate experience.

The fund is used to pay employees injured on the job until they are able to return to work, and should not be confused with unemployment insurance.

f. LIFE INSURANCE

If your key employees are sufficiently important to your restaurant, you may buy insurance on their life, payable to your restaurant. There are four basic types of life insurance:

(a) Term life

(b) Straight life

(c) Limited pay life

(d) Endowment life

To determine what is best for you, discuss your situation with an insurance company or broker.

Banks and other lending agencies often require key person insurance when you borrow money. For example, if you wish to borrow $50,000, the bank may require that you take out a $50,000 life insurance policy on one or more key employees of your restaurant, with the bank as beneficiary. In the event of accidental death of the insured, the bank would receive the face value of that insurance policy and could pay off any bank loan that you had.

Another type of key person insurance is a cross purchase plan where partners/shareholders in a restaurant agree to take out insurance on each other's lives. This allows the surviving owners to buy out the share of a deceased owner. For example, if A, B, and C each have an equal interest in a restaurant valued at $300,000, each will buy a $50,000 life insurance policy on the other two. If A dies, then B and C will each receive $50,000 and the combined amount of $100,000 will be enough to buy A's share of the restaurant.

When an insurance policy (other than term life) has been in effect for a few years it builds up a loan value. This loan value may be used to assist you in times of cash shortage since it can be assigned as collateral against loans. The full face value of the policy remains in effect during the period of the loan, subject to the amount of the outstanding loan.

Canadian readers can find further information in *Insuring Business Risks in Canada*, another title in the Self-Counsel Series.

21

ACCOUNTING RECORDS AND INTERNAL CONTROL

Prior to opening your new restaurant, you must establish an accounting system. It is in your own best interest to institute and maintain a complete record of all your restaurant's financing transactions.

The law requires that you keep certain accounting records for income tax purposes, and the better kept these records are the easier it will be to complete your restaurant's year-end tax return and take advantage of tax saving possibilities like depreciation on furniture, fixtures, equipment, and your building if you own it.

Well-documented accounting records will support the accuracy of your tax return. If your records are incomplete and do not allow you, for example, to calculate your taxable profits, the tax department may use methods of calculation that require you to pay more tax than you would if you kept proper records.

The actual books or records you keep will depend on the size, nature, and scope of your restaurant. Unless you have a background in accounting, you will probably want your accountant to set up an accounting system for you. However, the more daily routine recordkeeping you do for yourself, leaving only the month-end work for your accountant, the less your accountant's cost will be.

In addition, you would probably be wise to have your accountant prepare your tax return since he or she will be up to date on the most recent tax regulations and can help reduce the amount of tax your restaurant has to pay.

a. BASIC ACCOUNTING INFORMATION

Some of the basic information that any business needs to have a record of includes:

(a) Sales (sometimes called revenue) by the day, week, and month, and further broken down into cash or credit (by type of credit card if necessary), and by department (food and beverage), and even by menu item. Credit records are necessary to determine the amount of accounts receivable (money owed to you) at any particular time. Electronic registers can readily provide much of the detail concerning sales without extensive paperwork.

(b) Operating expenses by type (for example, purchases, supplies, rent) in total by sales period, and even by department. In addition, unpaid expenses at any time need to be known since these form your accounts payable.

(c) Payroll is a major expense for most restaurants. Legal requirements determine the detail that you must record. In particular, payroll withholdings for various levels of government must be properly documented.

(d) Inventory should be taken at least annually and, in certain restaurants, as frequently as monthly. Inventory must be separated by type (food and beverage). Electronic sales registers can often be used to record reductions in inventory as a result of a sale.

For all sales and expenses it is important that you keep all documents supporting any transactions. These documents include sales checks and register tapes; purchase invoices and/or receiving reports; canceled checks for both operating expenses and payroll; and receipts or memos for cash pay outs not otherwise supported by an invoice or check.

If you do wish to set up your own accounting records with minimal help from an outside accountant, see *Basic Accounting for the Small Business*, and *Understanding and Managing Financial Information*, two other titles in the Self-Counsel Series.

b. CASH RECEIPTS

Your accounting system should be established so that it gives you good control over cash receipts.

Good cash handling and internal control procedures are not only important to the restaurant owner or manager, but also to the employees involved since a good system will show that employees have handled their responsibilities correctly and honestly.

All cash receipts should be deposited intact each day in the bank. A deposit slip stamped by the bank should be kept as your receipt. If all cash received each day is deposited daily, no one who handles it will be tempted to "borrow" cash for a few days for personal use.

It also ensures that no payments are made in cash on invoices. If this were allowed, a dishonest employee could make out a false invoice and collect cash for it.

Employees who handle cash (and other assets such as inventories) should be bonded. In this way, losses are less likely to occur since the employee knows he or she will have to answer to the insurance company if shortages arise.

c. CASH DISBURSEMENTS

For minor disbursements that have to be handled by cash, establish a petty cash fund. You should put enough cash into this fund to take care of about one month's transactions. The fund should be the responsibility of one person only. Payments out of it must be supported by a receipt, voucher, or memorandum explaining the purpose of the disbursement.

When the cash fund is almost used up, the supporting receipts, vouchers, and memoranda can be turned in and will be your authority to replenish the fund with cash up to the original amount. Receipts, vouchers, or memoranda turned in should be stamped "paid," or canceled in some similar way, so that they cannot be reused.

All other disbursements should be made by check and supported by an approved invoice. All checks should be numbered in sequence. Checks should be prepared by you or a responsible person, but that other person should have no signing authority.

As checks are prepared, the related invoices should be canceled in some way so that there is no possibility of them being fraudulently reused. Any checks spoiled in preparation should be voided in some way so that they cannot be reused.

d. BANK RECONCILIATION

One control that is necessary in a good internal control system is a monthly bank reconciliation. At each month's end, obtain a statement from your bank showing each daily deposit, the amount of each check paid, and other items added to or subtracted from the bank balance. The canceled (paid) checks should accompany this statement. You should ensure, through the reconciliation, that your figure agrees with the bank's figure.

To ensure control, the bank reconciliation should not be carried out by the person who records cash receipts or disbursements, otherwise the reconciliation could be faked to cover theft.

e. CREDIT

Most credit that your restaurant is likely to be involved with will be from national or international credit cards. Before accepting any of these credit cards, you must make necessary arrangements with the credit card issuer.

The most popular credit cards are Visa, MasterCard, American Express, Diners Club, and Carte Blanche. When sales are made on credit cards, you are assured of full collection of those sales (assuming the credit card has not been blacklisted), less the credit card company charge.

Visa and MasterCard are bank credit cards, and sales slips made out using those cards can be deposited just like cash the next day in the bank. With nonbank credit cards you might not collect the cash for two or three weeks even if you send in the credit card sales slips promptly. Therefore, your employees should be encouraged to accept bank credit cards rather than the others if a customer has both.

Sales commission paid by you to the credit card issuer can be as high as 6% of the sale. The actual charge varies according to the volume of sales. Most restaurants pay the higher rates, although you should realize that, since the various credit card companies are in competition, the rates may be negotiable to a degree.

22
CONCLUSION

Starting and running a restaurant is not easy. To be successful, your restaurant needs good planning and a lot of hard work. This book gives you a head start in planning — the hard work is up to you.

It may help to remember that your restaurant will reflect you. When you first had the idea of opening a restaurant, it probably wasn't the financial statements and staff training you thought about — it was the decor, good food, and character of your dream restaurant.

Those characteristics, which grow out of your own taste, good judgment, and personality, are what will create a memorable atmosphere for your customers. Your good food and good service will reflect your own ideas and goals.

This atmosphere that you create will lessen the tediousness of daily operations and problems and put the fun into running your own restaurant.

This book is a guide to help you understand the details required for the "behind the scenes" success of starting your own restaurant. The information here will enable you to worry a little less about the details as your restaurant gets off the ground and enjoy that atmosphere a little more.